PRAISE FOR
# Shattering the Perfect Teacher Myth

"'A questioner is driven by wonder, but a doubter is blinded by limits.' This quote from Aaron not only struck a chord but it is an excellent summary of this book. Grounded in building relationships with those you serve, while also being a continuous learner in our journey as educators, Aaron reminds us what is important in education while pushing us to be better in our respective roles so that we create a legacy that lasts long past our time in education."

—**GEORGE COUROS**, author of *The Innovator's Mindset*

"Aaron Hogan speaks straight from the heart with power behind his words. This book moved me. It made me want to be better, to try harder, and to thrive more at every aspect of my career. If you read any book this year, it should be this one!"

—**TODD NESLONEY**, co-author of *Kids Deserve It!*

"More than a book, *Shattering the Perfect Teacher Myth* contains the new DNA of teaching, learning, and professional growth. Woven into the pages are unassuming ideas and thoughtful stories that elicit hope. Aaron Hogan has managed to craft a series of chapters that feel more like mile markers leading towards the next best version of myself as an educator, and for that I'm ever indebted."

—**BRAD GUSTAFSON**, principal and author of *Renegade Leadership*

"If you've ever found yourself spinning and drowning amongst all the demands in teaching to a point you are just trying to survive, then this book is a must! The beauty of *Shattering the Perfect Teacher Myth* is that Aaron has reached out his hand to support you past the surviving mode and into an energetic life of thriving. It's a dream come true to get your life back while making a huge impact!"

—**LAVONNA ROTH,** international speaker and creator/founder of Ignite Your S.H.I.N.E.®

"Aaron takes us on a compelling journey, reminding us why we *gladiate* for our students. This book is a convergence of hope and perseverance for our profession."

—MARLENA GROSS-TAYLOR, founder of EduGladiators.com

"Aaron Hogan reminds us in *Shattering the Perfect Teacher Myth* that the most important role we have as educators is to support others in becoming better people, especially our students. For those of you who have ever read a post from his blog, you will not be disappointed. What sets Aaron's writing apart is his genuine storytelling, honest reflections and practical examples that we can immediately adopt as a guide to help us move past our struggles and give us the confidence that we can not only do better for our students, but be better for them everyday ... every day."

—JIMMY CASAS, author, speaker, leadership coach, and senior fellow at International Center for Leadership in Education

"Educators who THRIVE are not only passionate about their work but equipped to go beyond the ordinary. Aaron offers encouragement and insight for everyday practitioners to grow in their craft and find support beyond their 4 walls."

—JEFF VEAL, co-founder of LeadUpChat

"Perspective is important. It affects how we look at students, parents, teachers and leaders. In *Shattering the Perfect Teacher Myth,* Aaron Hogan helps educators focus on the new perspectives they need to move forward. Whether it's our approach to classroom management, district and building initiatives, teaching strategies and student expectations, Hogan helps educators seek new ways to meet their goals. Aaron is a very talented writer and it's clear he put his heart and soul into this book. More importantly, he offers impactful suggestions based on research and his experience as a teacher, which will help all teachers THRIVE."

—PETER DEWITT, Finding Common Ground blogger, *Education Week* and author of *Collaborative Leadership: 6 Influences That Matter Most*

"*Shattering the Perfect Teacher Myth* is one of the best books about teaching and learning I have read in years. It is practical, inspiring, and a book you will refer back to more than once. In this book, Aaron Hogan exposes many of the myths we face in education and argues passionately for replacing the "Myths We Believe" with "Truths That Will Let Us Thrive." He does so by offering strategic and practical ideas for thriving—not merely surviving—as an educator. Hogan reminds us why we went into education in the first place and equips us to become re-invested in our students, our schools, and ourselves. This book is a must read for classroom teachers and school leaders."

—Dr. Jeffrey J. Zoul, assistant superintendent for teaching and learning of Deerfield Public Schools District 109

"Regardless of your experiences this book speaks to you. We have all wanted more for ourselves. We have all doubted our abilities. We feel things because we have an innate desire to want to THRIVE for our students. Aaron Hogan reminds us how to THRIVE and provides applicable ways in which we can do it tomorrow."

—Matthew Arend, principal of Sigler Elementary School, Plano, Texas

"Aaron Hogan provides great insights and strategies for educational leaders to shift their thinking. Based on six key factors, THRIVE helps educators, at all levels, to address the myths and realities to make meaningful impact with students, parents, and the community. Hogan reminds me the power in not just surviving the day, but in choosing to THRIVE!"

—Dr. Neil Gupta, director of Secondary Schools, Worthington City Schools

"In *Shattering the Perfect Teacher Myth*, Aaron Hogan engages and inspires with his masterful storytelling. Through his narrative, he connects philosophy to practical applications that will resonate with educators. I found the questions that he poses throughout the book promoted deep self-reflection on my part."

—Mark McCord, principal of Stockdick Junior High School, Katy, Texas

"*Shattering the Perfect Teacher Myth* is a book that each educator should have in their professional library. Its reflective nature makes it a useful tool that can be referenced time and time again. All of the answers to our deepest issues begin by reflecting, and THRIVE is the beginning of this process."

—Dr. Sanée Bell, principal of Morton Ranch Junior High School, Katy, Texas

"Nowadays, when I buy a book I am looking for one of three things; stories that engage me, real-world examples that I can actually relate to or strategies that can be put into place tomorrow. With *Shattering the Perfect Teacher Myth*, Aaron has provided all three! Through honest reflection and artful storytelling, Aaron has not only inspired us to be better, he has shown us how."

—Jon Harper, EdLeader, blogger, and host of the BAM Radio podcast "My Bad"

"Aaron Hogan shares his own experiences to offer the perfect recipe for affirmation, encouragement, and self-reflection. *Shattering the Perfect Teacher Myth* is filled with authentic ways to help educators improve their practice and influence others in the process. It is a perfect tool for educators who are passionate about becoming a better version of themselves."

—Bethany Hill, lead learner of Central Elementary, Cabot, Arkansas

# SHATTERING THE PERFECT TEACHER MYTH

6 Truths
That Will Help You
**THRIVE**
as an Educator

**Aaron Hogan**

This book is available at special discounts when purchased in quantity for use as premiums, promotions, fundraisers, or for educational use. For inquiries and details, contact the publisher at books@daveburgessconsulting.com.

Published by Dave Burgess Consulting, Inc.

San Diego, CA

http://daveburgessconsulting.com

Cover Design by Genesis Kohler

Editing and Interior Design by My Writers' Connection

Library of Congress Control Number: 2017940079

Paperback ISBN: 978-1-946444-15-8

Ebook ISBN: 978-1-946444-16-5

First Printing: June 2017

# Contents

# Author's Note

I wrote this book for teachers, but it's not filled with all the answers. Why not? For one, I don't have them. For another, to assert that reading a chapter in a book—or even an entire book—will allow you to effortlessly transform your classroom is insulting to all the educators out there doing exceptional work.

No, this book is not for anyone in search of a quick fix. Instead, it's for the dreamers and the weary alike. It's for those teachers who have big ideas and for those interested in trying something new. It's for those teachers who are spent and those who are scared of change but tired of the same routine. It's for the teachers who aren't sure they can keep going, but who show up each day and give 110 percent to their students and colleagues.

In many ways, this book is a reminder to myself of the things I tend to forget when life gets hectic. I currently serve as an assistant principal at Cypress Grove Intermediate School in College Station, Texas, and my time with our fifth and sixth graders is wonderful. But when I approach my work passively, I slide into survival mode. I don't think that state is a product of my current reality. Before moving to Cypress Grove, I served as an English teacher and assistant principal across town at my alma mater, A&M Consolidated High School. I've been in education for almost a decade now, and I have learned that regardless of my position, campus, or my own level of experience, I need regular reminders to push (and keep) me out of survival mode. Being intentional about my work, my time, and my thinking provides those reminders.

For those teachers who are done with just trying to survive, for those who are ready to THRIVE, this book is an invitation, the start of a journey, the beginning of a quest. This book is for teachers who want to *make* a difference and *be* the difference—in their classroom, on their campus, in their district, and across their state.

This path we will walk together will have some rough spots. You might feel singled out, unsure of, or even challenged by some of the ideas we explore, but I suspect you're up for it. That's why you got into education in the first place.

I don't consider this to be the kind of book that is consumed in huge gulps. Instead, I recommend a methodical pace that allows time for reflection and conversation. I have included summary questions at the end of each chapter to help you wrestle with the many issues surrounding what it means to THRIVE in education today. Because I write in the margins of my books all the time, I have provided you ample space for notes. (If I were to move on to the next chapter without any space or time for reflection, you would too, right?) Now, I understand that there are some folks out there who can't stand to write in their books. If that's you, feel free to enjoy the "Blogging to THRIVE" guide on my website at **afhogan.com/TeacherMyth**. There, you'll find additional prompts, ideas, and suggestions to help you THRIVE.

I'm glad you're here. Let's get started!

# Are You Ready to THRIVE?

I believe most people love a good story. I know I always have. Good stories draw us in and make us feel hopeful. While they're unfolding, they can be scary, funny, exciting, and weird, but ultimately good stories teach us important lessons and inspire us to act. I don't know you, but chances are, if you're an educator, I know something about you. You likely had some inspiration. Maybe you had an amazing teacher you can still remember all these years later. That educator who empowered you, valued you, made you feel capable, and did it all without you even knowing it was happening. Maybe you had a less-than-perfect experience, and you're here to make school different for future students. Either way, you're here for the right reasons.

That's why most people get into education—to make a meaningful difference in the lives of others. That's the good story we all want to be part of—even if we might not have articulated it that way. We come wired for stories. Stories drive us to do more, want more, and achieve more. They're how we find our place in the world.

Sometimes, though, we educators buy into stories that simply aren't true. They sound true, and if we're not careful, we end up using them as excuses or as a way to beat up on ourselves. A kernel of truth may lie within many of these stories, but then the entire narrative gives way to fictional ideas that leave teachers wrestling with guilt and shame.

I often wonder if that's what's behind the big disparity between the initial hopes and dreams that motivated us to become educators and our current, more complicated (often less dreamy) reality. When I talk to many educators, the conversation quickly takes a negative turn. The focus is on things we can't control, frustrations that seem insurmountable. I don't think anyone gets started in education without the hope of making a difference, but some teachers sure seem to be living that story more than others. Why is that? Why do we start out with such lofty goals and end up spending our time doing all sorts of other things? Why do we give up? The obstacles facing the average teacher are numerous, but they can be overcome. Even in the face of all those odds, countless educators are still finding ways to make a lasting impact on their students.

A few years ago, I found myself at a crossroads. This was my reality: I worked in an incredible school district with incredible students, supportive families, and many of the advantages that are supposed to make it easy to make the magic happen in the classroom. Even with all of those resources, I often left school feeling defeated. I was discouraged because I wasn't meeting what I believed were the standards of a successful educator. Somehow, I had come to believe that a successful educator was one who ...

- Never had student discipline problems
- Effortlessly earned compliance from students
- Could problem solve in isolation
- Excelled by meeting existing expectations
- Had all the answers to everything
- Earned respect solely with grand gestures

And while all of these skills are certainly impressive, the more I think about them, the more I'm convinced they tell the wrong story. They are the myths of teaching—illusions, legends if you will—that far too many of us have internalized as reality. For me, each one of these myths has played a part in holding me back as a teacher. At first glance, each of these abilities seems perfectly reasonable. In many educational settings, they are encouraged or even expected. But when teachers focus their energies on meeting these unattainable goals, they merely survive. When teachers move past these myths and half-truths and embrace a new way of thinking, they thrive. And isn't that why we chose education? Isn't our dream to empower kids? I wholeheartedly believe most teachers want to launch students into the world with the ability to make change, imagine a new reality, and lead in a way that values others. To that end, I propose a new paradigm, a fresh mindset that values excellence in teaching as well as collaboration and compassion. We need a new standard by which to judge our performance, one that allows for experimentation, failure, and the occasional restart.

Before we jump into this new way of thinking, let me remind you of something you already know: This new mindset isn't magic, and it's not going to wipe away every struggle you will face as an educator. What it can do is help you control what you can control and clear up misconceptions. It can direct your focus to those issues that affect your classroom the most. It can move you beyond simply trying to be a memorable teacher to trying with everything you have to do right by the students in your care. It can leave you terrified and vulnerable and requires more courage than you imagined. So if your goal is to be forgettable, feel free to put down this book. If you want your students to have an experience in your classroom or on your campus that makes them into better people, *Shattering the Perfect Teacher Myth* is for you.

Here's where this book is headed:

## CHAPTER 1—TEACHING EXPECTATIONS

As teachers, we know it's important to have high expectations for students. That said, the way we respond when students don't know how to behave is radically different from our response when students fail to grasp academic concepts. Whether mastering long division or the ability to keep one's hands to himself, it's all about learning. We will look at how a few simple changes in your approach have the potential to help all of your students flourish.

## Chapter 2—Hook Your Students

The best teachers convince their students they have something valuable, exciting, and useful to teach them. Those same teachers also know they have to set the scene. Lacking the right conditions, the deck could be stacked against you all year. We will explore how to set up a classroom environment where students belong and feel part of a dynamic community.

## Chapter 3—Reject Isolation

There are so many ways teachers need one another, and yet so much of our day is spent away from the other adults with whom we work. We will dig into the reasons for collaboration, its benefits, and what shape that idea can take in your school.

## Chapter 4—Imagine It Better

So much in education remains static, but we have the power not only to reimagine school for our students, but also to live out those dreams for what education could be. In chapter four, we will spend some time considering what we really want our work to be about and craft a plan to move toward that goal.

## Chapter 5—Value Vulnerability

Many of us want change, but too many of us want that to happen in a safe, secure fashion. As school leaders, titled and otherwise, we need to put ourselves—not our students—in the most vulnerable positions in our school. I believe, with renewed commitment, we can embrace vulnerability to make it safe for students to take risks, innovate, and create change.

## Chapter 6—Everyday Every Day

In our efforts to be educators who make an impact, we sometimes forget the value of our hallway conversations and everyday interactions with others. These moments matter greatly as the relational foundation that much of our work rests upon. We will outline some of the most valuable exchanges with students and colleagues that teachers can pursue each and every day on campus.

## Chapter 7—Inviting Others to THRIVE

Reflecting is crucial to our learning, but it's not likely to happen best in isolation. Blogging can draw you into a community of learners online and build your confidence in your professional learning. The journey is rewarding, but risky. In this chapter, we will create a plan for getting started (one of the biggest hurdles all bloggers face), and I'll share a few reasons I believe that you're more ready to start sharing your ideas than you may think.

## Chapter 8—Working with Survivors

The unfortunate reality is that we work alongside people who do not have the desire to THRIVE. Whether our colleagues are mired in the status quo or simply overwhelmed with the demands of our work, some have accepted that "just get me through the day/week/year" mindset of a survivor. Anticipating some of the common responses survivors share can be the difference in frustration and freedom in our work as we seek to THRIVE.

## Chapter 9—When We're Not Enough

When you do important work, it weighs on you when you don't see the success you hoped for. We must have a response when all of our strategies to meet students' needs fail to produce the desired results (and not one that involves us beating ourselves up). To THRIVE, we'll have to do better than avoiding self-criticism. To overcome circumstances that feel defeating, we need to know what gives us life and hope. We cannot afford to miss this.

## CHAPTER 1

# Teaching Expectations

Do the best you can until you know better.
Then, when you know better, do better.

—MAYA ANGELOU

## The **Myth** We Believe

The best teachers never have behavior problems from
their students.

## The **Truth** That Lets Us THRIVE

Behavior expectations can and must be taught.

One of the most harmful myths education has come to accept is that the best teachers never or rarely have behavior problems in their classrooms. It's simply not true, and I say we need to debunk this myth with the assertion that behavior expectations, like most any other concept, can and must be taught.

If you think about it, a teacher's response to an academic misstep often is radically different from her response to a behavior misstep. Students who struggle with academics are given time to review, relearn, and reassess until they master the content. Students who struggle with behavior are often deemed willfully disobedient, removed from the classroom, and assigned disciplinary consequences.

When we flip the script and apply our typical responses to behavior problems to academic problems, it's much easier to see the disparity. Consider this scenario: A student enters an English class to find it's that most dreaded of days—graded paper pass-back day. As one student receives his paper, the teacher begins criticizing his writing, pointing out mistakes, and saying, "You should have known better than to write your thesis that way!" What if the teacher went on to add, "That's the third time this month you've misspelled that word. What am I going to do with you?" before sending him to the hallway for his infraction?

What on earth would that student think if he were banished from the classroom for mistakes in his paper? My bet is that it's the same thing he would be thinking if he were sent out for the way he behaved.

Fortunately, thanks to good training, most teachers know this isn't the appropriate response to a poor academic performance. Somehow, though, it has become an acceptable way to address student behavior. And if I'm honest, if we're all honest, much of our response has to do with making incorrect and unfair assumptions about our students and their motives. Take a look at Figure 1.1 and consider how the expectations and assumptions differ regarding academics and behavior issues.

| Common expectations when students struggle... | |
| --- | --- |
| **With academics** | **With behavior** |
| • Anticipate mistakes<br>• Provide opportunities for practice and repetition<br>• Reteach when students miss the mark<br>• Reassess to determine what we need to revisit | • Assume willful disobedience<br>• Remove students from the learning environment<br>• Give them just one more chance<br>• Act surprised when this reaching didn't work |

*FIGURE 1.1*

Think about it—in an ideal world, we would know a great deal about our students. We would know their interests, details about their family life, and academic and behavioral history. We would know what books they like, what works for them, and what might really push their buttons. In an ideal world, we would not have to make any assumptions as we prepare to educate those students.

But life is rarely ideal. So we set out to do our best with a limited amount of information about our students. We try to get to know them as quickly as possible. We try our best and, in most cases, achieve remarkable results in rapid time. But teachers are human, and we get busy, tired, and irritated. At some point, we start making assumptions to fill the gaps in what we know about our students. They're made with the best of intentions—to serve students as well as we can as soon as we can—but they're assumptions all the same and often lead to unintended consequences.

I'm not going to spend time listing all of the ill-advised assumptions that teachers sometimes make. They're out there, and they're too common. What I'd rather focus on is what we can do differently. I believe, even with limited information about their students, teachers

3

can improve behavior in the same way they improve reading, writing, and comprehension skills: by simply tweaking their outlook.

## The Tricky Thing about Expectations

As a high school English teacher, I didn't think I needed to teach behavior. On the first day of school each year, I would put up a little timeline that showed eighth-grade and twelfth-grade graduation, and just to the right of center, a big X to mark where we were as we started junior year. I would then proceed to tell them that they were closer to graduation than they were to junior high and their behavior should reflect it. The final step in my oh-so-ingenious plan was to lay down the one classroom rule: *respect*.

The embarrassing part is that I was pretty proud of how this had gone. For about seventy-two hours, mostly due to that beginning-of-the-year honeymoon period and not my outstanding rules, things would go just fine. Then without any explanation, students would start showing less and less respect until behavior got out of hand. Crazy, right? How could my simple rule of respect—one single word—be dismissed so easily?

Turns out I had sold my students short on so many fronts. By not having any conversation about that complex term, I had missed the mark. And without any explanation of what graduation-day behavior should look like, they had little understanding of what I meant. Everyone was frustrated, and it was my fault. I was under the impression that if I posted rules and reviewed them in class on the first day, I had done all that was required. Maybe I had. But when it clearly didn't work, I still found myself returning to that list of posted rules. The bigger issue? I had no idea what to do next. As a teacher, that's a weird place to be. After all, we spend most of our time helping students understand new ideas and how to progress from skill to skill.

Eventually, though, I realized that my approach to behavior had failed because it wasn't based on teaching my students anything. I had honestly never thought about behavior and discipline in those terms. They're teenagers—surely they're old enough to know better, right? Wrong. For so many reasons, countless students reach high school without mastering basic behavioral expectations.

Over time, here's what I began to wonder: What might happen if I taught behavior expectations with my profession's best instructional practices? With academic content, teachers have numerous options. They start with what students know and build from there using models, repetition, and novelty to bring about learning. Why couldn't other teachers and I do the same with classroom and on-campus behavior?

Instead of looking at students as willfully disobeying all the good manners they had been taught, why not put a process in place to teach them our expectations for student behavior with the best practices often reserved for academics? Approaching behavior expectations this way could allow students to internalize our expectations better and longer.

## A Better Way

Back in my classroom, something had to change, so I identified a couple of behaviors and began to work on ways to review those expectations at a predictable rate. With my toughest class, we started with three basic expectations for class:

1. Be in your seat when class starts.
2. Listen when others, teachers and students alike, are talking.
3. Use language appropriate for school.

And I prepared lesson plans to teach these expectations. To seventeen-year-olds. It was weird.

But it worked. Not instantly, not without a few off days, not without the reappearance of frustration on both sides, but in the long run, it worked. Students learned more and felt more comfortable in our redefined environment, and I even had some of the quieter students who were fed up with their peers' poor choices tell me, "Thank you."

## Change at the Campus Level

In my role as an assistant principal at a high school, I had the opportunity to scale up this sort of teaching to the entire campus. At the beginning of one school year, we noticed students weren't picking up their trash between lunches. We thought they would know, especially as high school students, that trash pick-up was a rule, but it became clear we needed to explain and teach these students to master this particular behavior.

With our aim set on every student picking up his or her own trash after lunch, we calculated how long it would take our custodial staff to clean each of the sixty-plus table tops in the cafeteria between lunches and asked students to clean tables at that speed. We captured their efforts on video. The results were indeed entertaining and proved our point: The custodial staff can't collect trash from every table in time for students to sit at a table without trash on it, so everybody needs to chip in and pick up their own trash. We revisited this rule at key points—the beginning of the year, the first week of January, and the week after spring break—and with clearly defined expectations, students responded in the way we had hoped.

## Doing What's Right

It wasn't fun for me to realize I was the one who needed to make the big change after my beginning-of-the-year behavior speech, but it needed to happen. I'm glad it did, and so were my students.

I'd like to propose a better way. What if we committed to making these two assumptions about everyone we interact with at our schools?

- People are doing the best they can.

- When you know better, you do better.

I'm not asking you to be naïve or to live with your head in the sand. I know there are exceptions to nearly every rule, but this isn't a discussion about those outliers. This better way is about seeing your students in a new light on a daily basis. It's about granting grace to each and every person in our path—even if they're the fiftieth person doing that one thing that annoys us to no end. It's about letting the little things roll off our back, and it's about believing that kids can—and will—do better when we teach them to do just that.

Think about it. What if you approached each day with the attitude that your students are doing the best they can? What if you truly believed that your students will do better when they know better? What might be different tomorrow if you moved through your day with those two assumptions in place? How would you respond to misbehavior? How would you intervene when you noticed an academic struggle? How would you handle minor misconduct—the kind that easily becomes more annoying over time?

I'll be the first to admit that changing a habit isn't easy. But it's worth it. If teachers made this change, I think our schools would be different. I think they would be better.

Even if things aren't bad now—even if they're great now—defaulting to these two assumptions changes our posture as we educate students. Every kid deserves a fresh start with us each morning. Every kid deserves to learn in an environment that's going to push him and support him as he takes on new challenges. *Every kid deserves to be known.*

I believe we can be the teachers to imagine a better learning space and then make it a reality for our students. I believe we can change their worlds for the better by teaching them how to behave. And we must do it in the way that we, as experienced educators, know students learn—with models, repetition, patience, and review.

Beyond that, believing the best about students and setting them up for success in your classroom will help you earn the trust of your students, and that's a great place to start your story.

7

# Establish Clear Expectations

Here's the process along with a few starter ideas to move you in the right direction, whether you're an individual teacher or overseeing an entire campus.

- Establish clear, positively phrased expectations.
- Draft a list of memorable ways to teach these expectations and be sure to include models.
- Include a clear explanation of WHY these are your expectations.
- Estimate how often you will need to reteach this lesson.
- Create a timeline.
- Schedule reteaching reminders in a place you won't miss.
- Establish a list of signs that indicate when it's time to reteach these expectations.

It doesn't have to be a video. When we noticed that several of our most supportive students at athletic events had begun to be louder with their distaste of the opposing team than in their support of our own, we created a poster (Figure 1.2) to emphasize our expectations.

If you're a classroom teacher and are interested in trying out this idea, here are a few questions that might serve as a good point of departure for teaching discipline:

- What should students do when they hear the teacher's signal?
- What are the teacher's expectations when students enter the classroom?
- What are the teacher's expectations for electronic devices in the classroom?
- What should students do when they return from being absent?

**A&M Consolidated High School**

# Let's go Tigers!
Thanks for supporting our
Tigers as they compete!

At Tiger sporting events, remember that...

| TIGERS SUPPORT TIGERS | TIGERS TRUST OUR COACHES |
|---|---|
| Support our team instead of bashing the competition. | Trust our coaches to address issues with officials or referees. |
| **TIGERS DON'T GET PERSONAL** | **TIGERS ENJOY TIGER SPORTS** |
| Degrading comments will not be tolerated. | Stand tall, yell loud, and support your Tigers!!! |

*FIGURE 1.2*

If you want to take the school-wide approach, consider creating lessons to consistently establish these expectations at the campus level:

- Be on time to class.

- Follow the dress code.

- Eat food in the cafeteria (and only in the cafeteria).

- In the hallways, stop and listen if an adult speaks to you.

If you can't think of anything, the best way to generate ideas is to keep a list of good options for filling in the blank on this question: "You're X years old. I can't believe you still don't know how to _____!" When you find yourself asking this question, either aloud or in your head, it's time to reteach!

# Two Important Phrases

In general, Graham, my oldest, is a pretty good listener. He knows where the boundaries are and generally follows our set expectations. Even on his best days, there's always that wild card known as bedtime. It's easily the toughest time for Graham to keep it together. We have a decent routine, and he knows the expectations once we've tucked him in, but it's still a challenge. Each night, after we review his bedtime expectations, he repeats them back to me.

"Look at the stars (his night-light), be quiet, be still, no getting out of bed."

Everything but the last one, which was his addition to the list and one that gets no arguments from me, is phrased positively. But he just can't bring himself to consistently stay in bed when it's time.

One night, after a few days of unsuccessful attempts to get Graham to sleep quickly, he just nailed it. It was one of those things where you forgot that you were worrying about it because he just took care of business and drifted off to sleep. I was so excited that I peeked into his room, startled the little guy, and found him looking right at me—half-asleep, half-awake—and I leaned in to tell him that I was proud of him for choosing to go to sleep so quickly. He smiled, asked for a hug, and as I left the room, he whispered for me to come back. As I leaned over, he said, "Can you tell Mom what you said to me?"

"You want me to let Mom know I told you that I was proud of you, don't you?" I asked.

And with the biggest smile on his face, he nodded and hugged me as tight as his four-year-old arms would allow. It's sweet to know that he saw his dad was proud of him, and as much as that seemed to fill him up, I think it did more for me.

*Then there's that other important phrase.*

A few nights later, Graham and I circled in conversation until the discussion ended with one of those the-adult-makes-the-rules-not-the-four-year-old declarations. To make my point, I raised my voice and ended the conversation with some finality, again reviewing his bedtime expectations.

I'm really not one to get agitated. Ask my wife; ask the folks I work with. They'll all tell you I'm the last guy to raise my voice about anything. But here, I did.

Feeling a bit sheepish about it all, I went back in to check on Graham about ten minutes later, and he asked me to sit on the bed. When I did, he pulled on my arm to draw my head closer to his, and he whispered, "Dad, say you're sorry."

And, of course, I did.

And in the sweet way that a child knows, he reached up, hugged me, and offered a four-year-old's restoration.

Not long after that, I began to wonder how much more good could be done if we made sure these phrases—*I'm proud of you* and *I'm sorry*—were said more often.

What if the fourteen-year-olds in our school heard those two phrases when the appropriate time came? What if students could expect to see adults own their mistakes and apologize, providing a glimpse of the vulnerability that comes with personal growth?

What if students knew that they would hear genuine praise from their teachers? How would it help them to know there are people at school who are proud of what they've accomplished, proud of the risks they've taken, and proud of the character they've shown?

We have more opportunities than we realize to use these two important phrases. So keep them in mind, and don't miss your chance!

# THRIVE
## SUMMARY QUESTIONS

Think about your classroom or campus. What is one behavior you are constantly correcting? How could you reset your expectations? What can you do to reteach those expectations to students through-out the year?

If you knew you would have visitors in your class or on your campus, what would you address with your students before the visitors arrived? Why not tackle that now?

Look back at the "Common Expectations" graphic (Figure 1.1) from earlier in this chapter. What surprises you about this information? Considering that comparison, what are some changes you could make to your teaching practices?

Select three experienced teachers on your campus and observe them in the classroom. Record your observations about how they handle behavior struggles.

*Teacher 1:*

*Teacher 2:*

*Teacher 3:*

Write each of those teachers an encouraging note about how valuable their work is to their students and your school. Follow up with an encouraging note to yourself, emphasizing that it's normal for teachers to have students who regularly need redirection.

## CHAPTER 2
# Hook Your Students

And now that you don't have to be perfect, you can be good.

—John Steinbeck, *East of Eden*

## The **Myth** We Believe
The best teachers effortlessly earn compliance from their students.

## The **Truth** That Lets Us THRIVE
Compliance should never be our main goal. Engagement is the result of deliberate design, rapport developed with students over time, and an intentional search for inclusive classroom community.

**I'm one of the lucky ones.** My first teaching job wasn't one characterized by worst-case scenarios. The first day was rough—more on that later—but the year was free from many of the common ills that first-year teachers face. I was surrounded by an incredible group of teachers. They were (are) phenomenal people and fantastic educators; so good, in fact, they made teaching look easy. It seemed as if every time they spoke, students not only listened, but also hung on every word. I found it nothing short of amazing.

For the most part, I was passionate, eager, and fighting my introverted nature like a champ, but I still had zero minutes of teaching experience under my belt. No student teaching. No subbing. No nothing. *Nada.* I was overwhelmed by everything I didn't yet know and wondered how I would ever compare to my colleagues. Down the hall in every direction, teachers seemed to make magic happen. One could forge meaningful connections with her students faster than anyone I'd ever seen, and she never got rattled in class. It was almost unbelievable. Another teacher could get eighteen-year-old seniors, those I'm-way-too-cool-for-this types, to dance around a little "fire" she built in her room. (Because, of course, that's what awesome teachers do when teaching *Macbeth*.)

Another of those teachers taught AP English with what seemed like an encyclopedic knowledge of the texts. At the same time, he inspired students to think deeply about their role in social issues they were actually studying. Surely he had someone feeding him information as class was progressing, right? Then there was the teacher who was a master storyteller with a Mark Twain quote for every situation and a gift for imparting wisdom to students. There was the outspoken teacher with the drive to take on delicate discussions about the power of our words, the teacher who could get more growth out of sophomores in one year than most great teachers hope to see in two years, and the teacher who had the natural ability to connect with and challenge any student—freshmen or seniors, those who loved school and those who loved to hate school. And, finally, there was the teacher who could manage to get any kid in the building excited about poetry.

It's still mind-boggling when I look back and realize that these descriptions aren't exaggerations. In fact, I'm sure I'm selling them short. A&M Consolidated High School was, and still is, a fantastic place to teach. But from where I sat, as a new teacher, it all seemed so easy for them and so difficult for me. As a result, I spent a lot of time working hard to appear as if I wasn't doing just that. For some reason, I believed that if I could make it look easy, that would communicate a sense of success.

That's not exactly time well spent.

As I got to know these master teachers who taught in the English halls, I realized how much they had invested on the front end. As it turns out, developing teenagers into thoughtful readers and writers doesn't always happen all that easily. What had looked like natural perfection was actually the result of years of developing their craft.

I'd love to say that by Thanksgiving of that first year I figured this out. I didn't. I was arrogant and impatient, wanting to make the magic happen immediately. Instead of coming to terms with that, I vowed to fake it till I made it. In all honesty, it took a long time for me to realize that becoming a great teacher was its own unique learning process. But I did. I learned that it's not a teacher's job to be perfect. I learned that there are too many uncontrollable factors in a classroom—and in our students' lives—to guarantee a full slate of successful outcomes. I learned that teachers can put processes in place that will pave the way for healthy relationships and solid learning gains in their classrooms and across their campuses.

## What's Really Happening

These teachers I so greatly admired had figured this out. So what was their secret? They had learned to hook their students. It happened early, it stuck, and it lasted for the rest of the school year, with their students showing genuine interest in what they were teaching. For an educator, that's a great place to be, but I discovered that it doesn't happen overnight. It's the result of a great deal of planning and effort on the part of the thriving teacher. It's the result of taking time to identify those core values that will set the right tone for your school year. Failing to identify these key concepts can be disastrous for students and teachers because without them, communication and decorum break down—and that's when life in the classroom can get ugly.

## A WITCH HUNT

One of my favorite days in the classroom started off with a witch hunt. It was beautiful. We were starting Arthur Miller's *The Crucible*, which is ostensibly about the Salem witch trials, but offers a parallel critique of the way many Americans were treated when fears of communism drove what came to be known as the "Red Scare." Without giving you a long history lesson or dragging you through the play, you need to know the following about both events:

- Guilt was assumed instead of innocence.
- The accused could clear their names by admitting to wrong-doing—either practicing witchcraft or having communist sympathies or affiliations.
- Everything was handled publicly.
- Nobody was safe from accusation.
- If you defended someone, you were assumed to be involved in the nefarious behavior.

Before completing our previous unit, a partner teacher came to me and suggested we give students an experience of what it was like to live through the Red Scare or the McCarthy era. Ready with our plan, the day after our test for *The Scarlet Letter*, and scheduled to begin our work with *The Crucible*, I sent this email to myself.

> *Mr. Hogan,*
>
> *This weekend, I've gone back and forth about what to do about some of my classmates' behavior. I know for a fact that some of my classmates dishonestly prepared for the test at the end of last week. There's a list of answers to last year's questions circulating, and several students simply printed off that old list of responses. What's more frustrating is that they received higher scores than many of the people I studied with for the exam.* ████████████, ███████, *and* ██████████ *here all cheated on the test. I suspect that many others might have used that list of answers as well.*
>
> *I wish I had scored higher on the exam, but I'm not asking for any grades to be changed. I thought you should know what I know, though.*
>
> *Your student,*
>
> ████████████

I spoke with each of the three students, all girls, before their class began and told them I was going to accuse them of cheating on the test. All they needed to do was deny the charges and then publicly accuse another student of cheating. I was pumped!

Now, most of the time, I'm a pretty relaxed guy. I greet students in the hallway, talk about their activities, and enjoy the unstructured time. Not on this day. I was somber and withdrawn. I even had a couple of students ask me if everything was okay. I told them we would talk about it as soon as the bell rang, and boy did we!

I gave them a minute before I entered, walking slowly to the podium that was uncharacteristically at the front of the room with my email just waiting to be read.

"Guys, we have something we need to talk about. I received an email last night that I need to read for you. It seems that we've been a little too trusting with you guys, and that some students have chosen to take advantage of that trust. Here's what was sent to us last night."

And then I read the email, including the name of the student from that class period. After a dramatic pause, I looked up at the accused. All three were model citizens—well-liked by all and strong students too—and asked them what they had to say. Stone cold, these sweet girls began blaming other students, and it was on! Students vigorously defended each other, I accused many of being in cahoots with the suspected cheaters, and panic swept across the classroom.

I'm not the kind of guy who wants to traumatize my students, but this opening to our study of *The Crucible* provided a memorable experience of what it was like to be falsely accused. After about ten minutes, I began to let them in on the joke, transitioning the class from this crazy experiment to a serious discussion about how it paralleled the lives of the characters in *The Crucible* and those Americans who were accused of being communists.

At this point, we had built up enough trust that my students didn't start throwing stuff at me, but I suspect a few came close. On most days, witchcraft and communism can feel like ideas that are pretty far away from a sixteen-year-old's reality. Not on this day. My students felt the helplessness that the accused experienced. They knew the shock of seeing friends accused, and they saw how quickly irrationality could spread within a group based on a single lie.

I had a set of notes that said all that same stuff, but if I'd gone that route, I doubt my students would still come up to me and reminisce about that day. The exercise was so memorable, in fact, that we could never do it again. Everybody in school knew about it. I never had that happen on a notes day.

The odds are not great that *The Crucible* or the Red Scare are part of your course. But you don't need to do exactly what I did to make

Learning shouldn't happen *to* our students. It's an experience in which they should take part.

your class memorable. The key is engaging students and drawing them in with dynamic learning experiences. Learning shouldn't happen *to* our students. It's an experience in which they should take part. When that happens, the magic follows. I didn't have even a glimmer of an issue with misbehavior during the experience or the debrief that followed. On that day, learning was fun. It was interesting. It was experiential. And it stuck. Mission accomplished.

## Design for Experience

It's our duty and often lots of fun to search for those opportunities to pull students into a powerful learning experience. For the most part, I was unsuccessful in pulling those off. I just didn't think outside the normal constraints enough to bring those ideas to life, but in hindsight, I can see how much my students and I would have benefited from it.

One of those opportunities just waiting to be explored is classroom design. If you're a teacher with your own classroom and the freedom to get creative, this can be a wonderful way to try your hand at thinking outside the proverbial box. There's no law that dictates your classroom must have all thirty desks pointed in the same direction and be decorated with nothing but educational posters. (Many experts out there say the opposite!)

So what can you do to design your classroom for more experiential learning? First, think about where your students hang out and learn on their own outside of school. Depending on the grade you teach, they might do a considerable bit of learning in a coffee shop, at a Lego table, on a playground, or in a sandbox. Each of these could be tough to pull off in your classroom, but there are elements that are worth considering for inclusion in your classroom design.

## SET THE SCENE

Before your students ever learn anything from you, they will start learning about you. They'll make assumptions based on their first interactions with you. Your classroom design is one of those indicators that will help students answer the pressing question, "How is this year going to go?"

It won't take them long at all to decide who they think you are and how they believe the year is going to go. That's not news to any experienced educator. But if we move forward doing what we've always done without considering how we can hook our students so we have their full attention in class, we've missed an important opportunity.

One of my favorite examples of innovative classroom design is in my own school district. When Chad Lehrmann, a teacher at College Station High School, got the always-exciting news that he would be changing rooms over the summer, he took the opportunity to make the most of the switch. Chad decided to give his classroom a coffee shop feel. The seating is a near replication of a coffee house lounge, the lighting is lower and often from lamps instead of the standard fluorescent classroom lights, and there's the unmistakable aroma of coffee wafting through the air. The most profound difference, though, is in the way the students interact with one another. Chad would be quick to downplay his role as facilitator or classroom designer, but the design of his classroom is helping him turn everyday conversations into learning experiences. Instead of being a neutral element of the environment or even a barrier to conversation, his classroom design paves the way for him and his students to thrive.

## WIN THEIR ATTENTION

The beauty of this discussion about classroom design is that a few small tweaks can go a long way (a good thing since education is not a field known for making fast changes). You don't need LEGO tables or 3D printers or virtual-reality viewers or a coffee shop to capture the attention of your students. Something as simple as decorating your room in a unique way that fits you, rearranging the seating, or adding music to the space can pique your students' interest in a new way. Whatever changes you make to your classroom's design, keep in mind that you must embrace the reality that you will have to work to win your students' attention. (By saying must, I'm assuming you want to thrive. If not, design your classroom for apathy, and that's exactly what you'll get.)

Classroom design is a good place to start, but capturing students' attention goes well beyond the placement of your chairs and tables. Our lessons, too, must be designed with care. Students today are accustomed to instant gratification. They have had 24/7 access to television, movies, and modes of communication. They don't hesitate to click on to the next best thing when they tire of what's in front of them. It's no wonder that being in a classroom for an extended time period often leaves them wanting more.

Don't make the mistake of thinking that you might make an impact on kids this year. In every case, with every student, you will make an impact by either upsetting the status quo or continuing to make school about test scores and compliance.

In *Teach Like a Pirate*, author Dave Burgess challenges educators to raise the bar by asking these two questions:

- "If your students didn't have to be there, would you be teaching to an empty room?"
- "Do you have any lessons you could sell tickets for?"

Honestly, his challenge scares me. I don't know if I've ever led a faculty meeting I could sell tickets to. But I need to push for that. We all do (you know, if we want to thrive).

Just remember—the specifics of how you design your classroom aren't nearly as important as your willingness to be intentional and creative in improving your students' learning environment.

# Invisible People

All the experiential learning and classroom design in the world isn't likely to stimulate every single student. We have too many unique individuals in our classrooms to pretend that even the best solutions always meet the needs of every student we serve. In reality, there are invisible people in your classroom and in your school right now.

No, they're not ghosts haunting the hallways. They are students who, like the unnamed narrator in Ralph Ellison's *Invisible Man*, are "invisible, understand, simply because people refuse to see" them for who they are. They're largely unnoticed, many are compliant, and all are disconnected. Some of these students think this is the only way they'll ever experience school. After all, they missed the welcome-to-high school orientation, they're not sure who to talk to about sports or clubs, and their older siblings preceded them in living the invisible life, so why expect anything different?

They're in more of our classrooms than we'd guess. They are students who live in poverty, in affluence, and everything in between. They exist at, below, and above grade level, and they are rarely involved in school activities.

But how do we identify these invisibles? At your school, do you know who's involved and who isn't? Could you put pen to paper and create a list of students connected to this sport or that club? Do you know how your students would answer the question, "Who are your people on this campus?" I believe it's time we start finding ways to ensure that we're reaching out to all of the students on our campuses.

You'd be hard pressed to find an educator who would argue against the positive benefits of relationships. Yet if we truly believe that relationships and a feeling of belonging at school are vital to student success, we need to step up and take action on our students' behalf. Consider the students who were new to your campus this year. Who struggled? Who continued to struggle to meet academic and behavior expectations after spring break? What needs to change in your models and instruction as you teach students to expect better of themselves on your campus?

As you think through those questions, also consider the best ways to prepare students who are new to your campus to meet those expectations. What have you done so far to identify new students who might struggle to get connected? What are some of their greatest needs? What can you do to help them connect to a positive group or activity in your school community? Whatever your response to those questions, resist the easy path of believing the rumors about that next incoming group and keep an open mind.

As a high school leadership team, we invested considerable time into brainstorming options for a number of different populations among our incoming ninth-graders. We talked about how to serve students who struggle academically due to minimal attendance and discipline issues. We explored how to reach students who might have trouble meeting the behavior expectations at our school. We discussed how to intervene before high school began, how to establish positive relationships, and how to provide a taste of academic success for students who had traditionally struggled. Most of all, I'm thrilled that our success in certain initiatives generated further conversations about helping more students—particularly the invisible ones—in future years.

We actively search for these kids, and we learn along the way. I encourage you to do the same. If you have successful programs in place at your school, I applaud you, but try not to let them become an excuse for not starting new conversations about how to help those invisible students on your campus.

# Be Good

I've said it before, but I'll repeat it here: Teachers don't need to be perfect. It's not an attainable goal, and you'll waste valuable time trying to get there. What teachers can do is focus on those practices that will hook our students and draw them in to a memorable learning experience. I suggest reflecting on this challenge every six weeks, brainstorming ways to do the following:

- Redesign one element of your classroom
- Provide your students with a creative learning experience
- Connect with students who are invisible

Remember, thriving isn't about being able to turn on a dime and fix all of your school's problems overnight. I certainly don't have that kind of plan to offer, and I would be wary of anyone who does. Thriving, I believe, is about committing to a process that will produce growth over time. It's about the long haul. I realize now that commitment is what I recognized in those teachers I so admired at the start of my career. What I perceived to be perfection was simply expertise that had been carefully honed over time by a group of educators determined to hook their students to develop them into thoughtful readers, writers, and thinkers, and send them out to do good in the world. I have no doubt that you can do the same.

Go forth and be good.

# THRIVE
## SUMMARY QUESTIONS

What aspects of your classroom are designed for compliance?

How can those be shifted or reimagined to also foster community?

How many of your students are hooked into clubs or sports on campus? Try listing as many as you can think of.

What are some ways you can engage some of the disconnected students in your classroom?

What content do you teach that could be reworked into an engaging experience for students?

What are some of your personal interests that you could share with your class to engage disconnected or invisible students?
List some of those interests here:

Which of these interests might appeal to teenagers?

Try starting a discussion in class about the value of getting involved at school. Observe and record some of the reactions and build on that information.

Like students, teachers don't learn by osmosis; they must be taught and allowed to learn and progress over time. Think about your own experience with compliance and student engagement. What do you wish you could go back and tell yourself at the beginning of this week? This year? Your career?

Select a younger teacher, ask how things are going, and share what you wish you had known. Try completing this checklist when interacting with this colleague:

- [ ] Send this teacher a few encouraging notes
- [ ] Check on this teacher during the day
- [ ] Praise something specific about this teacher's performance
- [ ] Engage this teacher through an online platform
- [ ] Share some of your favorite professional websites or online resources with this teacher
- [ ] Offer the teacher time to work through work frustrations

## CHAPTER 3
# Reject Isolation

Failure we can do alone.
Success always takes help.

—Simon Sinek, Together is Better

## The **Myth** We Believe
The best teachers can solve their problems in isolation.

## The **Truth** That Lets Us THRIVE
Educators thrive in community with their peers and their students; the most meaningful change is the result of collaboration.

# My first day in the classroom was terrible. It

wasn't bad in the I'm-suppposed-to-say-I-was-bad-because-I-can-tell-I've-grown-since-then-but-I-don't-want-to-boast sense, either. It was bad. I had first period off, which was great because I'm not a morning person. On this first day, however, it left just enough time for the knots in my stomach to tighten into even more knots. As I was walking back into the main building to get some water, the power went out. I was going to get a reprieve! We couldn't have school with the power out, right? Wrong.

My department head walked around the corner, and instead of telling me she would see me the next day, she said in a positive, supportive manner that they were working on getting power restored as quickly as possible, that I would do a great job, and that she would be excited to hear how my first day went. Awesome.

So I went back to my portable and begin to put on this ridiculous costume I decided to use during my *first minutes of teaching ever.* On top of my uncomfortable-shirt-and-tie teacher clothes, I donned a rain jacket. On top of that, a graduation robe. The plan was to start with the end—graduation, of course—then explain that I would be their guide on the path toward this goal, and then end with the realization that I was the teacher who could get them there. By the end, they would realize how much they were going to love me, the class, reading, books, and the very process of learning! Right. Here's what actually happened: I put everything on and began to sweat. A lot. Blame it on first-day jitters or not having any power, and therefore no air conditioning, in late August in central Texas, or anything else you want. Regardless of the reason, I was sweating profusely by the time the students arrived. It was not fun and certainly was not how I had pictured starting my teaching career.

I'll spare you all the soggy details and offer this summary: I pushed through the entire morning of classes packed with more than thirty high school juniors in a stuffy portable with no power to play the slide show I had prepared, the one accompanied by music I had so carefully chosen to convey I was going to be *that* teacher, *that* adult with whom they could easily relate. By lunchtime, I was pondering what else I could do with my life. The morning left me embarrassed, frustrated, and intimidated by the prospect of going back for day two. But I did go back, and things got better.

## My Worst Decision

I made a lot of bad decisions that first day, but the worst decision from my first day didn't have anything to do with what was happening or not happening in the classroom. My worst decision was to sit silently by my peers at lunch while I felt so stressed. Right there sitting next to me were the people who could help me most, people who later became my friends and taught me how to teach. I just sat there and beat myself up. The story ends well, but on that day I felt like I needed to turn everything around all on my own. I had convinced myself that was my only option because it was what the best teachers would do, and that's what I wanted to be.

The single best thing that happened that day was that a nearby teacher brought me a Coke, and said, "How's it going?" and talked to me about how things were, in fact, going. Don't get me wrong, ditching the rain jacket and the graduation robe helped tremendously, but engaging with my colleague instead of retreating was my smartest move.

## Thankful and Restless

I'm incredibly thankful for that teacher and her willingness to sit with me on her first day back, which we all know to be exhausting. Even if it's the best, most welcome sort of exhaustion, it's absolutely draining.

That solved my day one problem, but it didn't address the motivation that drove me so far out of my comfort zone. You see, I believed

I could make the magic happen all in those first fifty minutes. I had thought about what I wanted for my students and came to the conclusion that I had to become someone else to make that happen. I had convinced myself I wasn't the guy for that job.

What a lie.

Sure, I felt woefully unprepared for all sorts of things that first day of school, but I was the one they hired to do the job. Not someone with years of experience or the best answers or even much confidence. Me.

As I think back, even before that first day began, I had set myself up to fail. I had told myself repeatedly and come to believe that it was vital to establish a lasting bond with my students on that first day. To miss that mark was to fail.

# Eight Ways to Reject Isolation

Most teachers would agree that professional isolation is not ideal. But, in reality, it can be extremely difficult to shake up a regular routine or step out of a comfort zone to engage a colleague in new ways. Here are a few ideas that will help you connect with the educators who are working hard in your building as well as those who are fighting to make school a great place for students online.

**In your building**

1. Ask about family.
2. Explore professional interests.
3. Gather input before making decisions.
4. Ask for critical feedback.

**Using social media**

5. Leverage the power of social media for your benefit.
6. Interact with experts/bloggers.
7. Find the places where educators are gathering.
8. Make friends.

# Create Meaningful Change

The more I think about it, the more I believe our legacy as educators lies in building community over time. The programs put in place will change. Initiatives will pass. Teaching trends will fall in and out of fashion. But the relational impact we have will outlast us by far. If we want to be teachers who make a difference, we must first create a space where students can learn alongside us as well as their peers. First, we must resolve to do it together—as a team, a village, a family of professionals—instead of on our own. Next, we commit to being real and knocking down those barriers that we put up to feel safe and in control. We must be willing to be vulnerable and learn what we do not know. Finally, we must act—and help each other back up when we fail—in the best interests of students.

# Get Connected

There's a lot of talk these days about how worthwhile it is to be a connected educator. I'm one of those people doing that talking. I'm trying my best to be out there doing what I can to help people get connected. I might even be annoying some people, but there's good reason for that. Nothing has had a greater impact on me as a professional educator than getting connected online, and I want my colleagues to know!

Take Twitter, for instance. It's a powerful social media platform, and I not only want teachers to know why they should use it, but also how to use it. Too often, that piece of the conversation is oversimplified or neglected altogether. Just create a profile, log on, find a few educators to follow, and you're done, right? It's not that simple. The truth is I jumped on Twitter in 2009 and did nothing with it for five years. I was there for all the right reasons. I truly believed Twitter could be a space where educators reject isolation, celebrate successes, and grow professionally together. I simply didn't know how to proceed. I looked at tweets from famous people, tweeted about thirty times, and gave up. Here's some of what I wish I had known at the time.

# WHAT TO DO WHEN YOU GET THERE

My first issue was that I had no idea how to move forward after I downloaded the Twitter app. I'd tweet about silly things I'd seen, about the Astros, or about Texas A&M football, and none of it ever seemed to matter much to me or to anyone else out there—especially educators. Nobody had ever told me there was a better way. I had no idea there were educators gathering on Twitter for chats—and in growing numbers—to discuss ideas that would challenge me to consider new perspectives as I grew professionally.

Eventually, I figured this out by following a wide range of people. My process wasn't scientific. If I saw people saying something I liked, something I found encouraging or challenging, I followed them. Pretty quickly I began to trust a few voices, and I would always take a look at the people they followed. Not everyone was a good fit, but I always found someone with something interesting to say.

I also learned to check out other people's lists. I have a list that includes a bunch of people who push my thinking (twitter.com/aaron_hogan/lists/education-inspiration/members). You can also find tons of great educators on Fridays by looking at the Follow Friday hashtag (#FF) posts of those you follow and trust. You can also compile lists of educators from certain fields or educators who specialize in certain issues.

I love the advice Ryan McLane and Eric Lowe, authors of *Your School Rocks . . . So Tell People!*, shared at a recent conference: Whether you're sharing for your school or for yourself, with each post, do your best to engage, inform, and inspire others. That's as succinct a summary I can find for what we as educators should be about online. If we accomplish that, we're heading in the right direction. After I started following people who challenged, encouraged, and inspired me, I realized

# When educators join forces, offer support, and hold each other accountable, we all get better.

Twitter chats were going to be pivotal in my online learning experience. A Twitter chat is a conversation based on a particular hashtag at a set time. They often happen weekly, and they usually last for thirty minutes to an hour. More than anything, these chats are my favorite place to connect with new educators and try new ideas.

Want to find a Twitter chat for you? Need to learn how to participate in a Twitter chat? Don't know what TweetDeck is? Find those resources and more at afhogan.com.

Now that I've dumped a good bit of information on you, here's more about my journey into the Twitter chat world. My first interactions with Twitter chats weren't really interactions at all. I was there, but I didn't say anything. I was a lurker. I was there reading the questions and the responses, and on rare occasions, I felt bold enough to mark a few of the tweets as *favorites* (now rebranded as *likes*).

I watched what must have been months of #TXeduchat before finally jumping in. It was a little scary, but mostly great. If you've not been in a chat before, it's a great place to shift your online learning into the next gear. Here are two things I learned that I hope you'll remember: You have more to say than you realize, and your work is worth sharing.

I love what speaker and *Teach Like a PIRATE* author Dave Burgess says about the importance of being bold enough to jump in and share what you know: "If what you know/have can help educators, you have a moral imperative to get good at sharing it." When educators join forces, offer support, and hold each other accountable, we all get better. The snowball picks up the best sort of momentum as it rolls, and the exchange of ideas is exhilarating.

Until it starts to feel like too much.

# THE BLESSING AND CURSE OF SO MUCH GOOD CONTENT

At first, you can read most of what is in your Twitter feed, but soon enough, all of those great ideas are going to become overwhelming in number. Twitter isn't designed to be a read-everything-that's-posted experience. If you try to treat it as such, you're going to drive yourself a little crazy. But there is excellent content out there you don't want to miss, so what do you do?

Enter Nuzzel. Nuzzel is an app that aggregates all the blogs and articles shared by the people you are following. It's like a best-of list that's automatically updated daily with what's new and notable. And it's awesome. I use it every single day—zero exaggeration. It's the first place I go when I have a few minutes to engage, especially when I come across a surprise gap in my day.

The app is slick, the posts are customized, and it's easy to share what I like with others right from the app. You can even check out the feeds of other Nuzzel users. Let's be clear—I'm not on the Nuzzel payroll. It's just a phenomenal tool that helps you stay in the know when time is at a premium, which is every weekday of the school year, right?

## So Many Tweets, So Little Time

It happened again last week. Someone familiar with my Twitter feed asked me if I ever slept. It doesn't bother me. Really, it's a conversation starter. As I look through my feed, I often come across people who binge post—you know, tweet all twenty-five resources they have in a ten-minute time period. While that's certainly one way to share, it can annoy some of your followers. Still, it's a shame for something as minor as posting frequency to get in the way of sharing good content. I, and many others, schedule our tweets to appear at different times of the day. It helps me find time away from my phone and social media while still sharing ideas that stretch and refine me.

My go-to app for scheduling my posts is Buffer, a tool that integrates seamlessly with Nuzzel, which allows you to push posts into a queue to be shared at specific times. It's another app I use daily, and it helps me balance being a connected educator with being a fully engaged husband, dad, and friend.

## INTERNET FRIENDS

My wife thinks it's hilarious that I have what she calls "Internet friends." You see, at some point, my connections online reached a point where it was more appropriate to call these folks my friends than someone I followed on Twitter. I realize it might sound a little odd. Some people don't consider the Internet a place to strike up friendships, but I can truly say I have found a group of friends there. I've asked their advice, listened to their struggles, shared in victories and in hardships, and I've even had them and their families over for dinner. Those relationships that developed quickly and reach beyond the surface level started on Twitter, but were cultivated further through face-to-face interactions and conversations using my final app suggestion—Voxer.

> The real value of pursuing professional growth on social media is the people you will meet. They're amazing.

Voxer is a push-to-talk, walkie-talkie app that many educators are using to find deeper connections than communication via Twitter's 140 characters allows. Even if you could send a longer text, there's something different about hearing the passion or heartbreak in someone's voice as they talk about wanting to make a difference in the lives of students and teachers. For me, Voxer provides a space for that. It's how I start and end each day at work. As a result, I'm connected to people across my district and across the country in ways that otherwise wouldn't be possible.

Remember, the real value of pursuing professional growth on social media is the people you will meet. They're amazing. They will challenge, support, encourage, and inspire you, and you will return the favor. My greatest hope is that more educators will jump online and find what they need to excel. My challenge to you is to find someone in your building as the year starts and encourage them to go online. Learn from my mistakes and start sharing today.

# THRIVE
## SUMMARY QUESTIONS

How do you share what you are learning as a professional?

List three people you could share professional development ideas with on your campus or in your district.

1. _____

2. _____

3. _____

What successes and failures could you share with them?

Who are the people you can dive deep with as you grow as a professional? Get in touch with them—write a note, walk down the hall, tweet at them, Vox them, whatever—and thank them.

Who should you engage next on your campus? Make a list of a few people you would like to get to know. Make a plan and tell those educators you trust about that plan, so they can help keep you accountable.

Who are the teachers on your campus who are most likely to embrace professional isolation? List at least three people. What are some ways you can counteract this?

What systems and safeguards can you put into place to prevent this isolation from being so likely?

## CHAPTER 4

# Imagine It Better

We do not need magic to change the world,
we carry all the power we need inside ourselves
already: We have the power to imagine it better.

—J.K. Rowling

## The **Myth** We Believe

The best teachers excel by meeting
existing expectations.

## The **Truth** That Lets Us THRIVE

Teachers thrive when they dream big with the ways they
can upset the status quo and reimagine what's possible
for their students.

**W**hen you learned to ride a bike, it probably went a lot like this:

Got a bike.

Got unreasonably excited.

Slapped on some training wheels.

Learned to pedal.

Fell off. A lot.

Got better at the pedaling.

Continued to fall.

Got good enough to lose the training wheels.

Had someone run behind the bike to help with still more falling.

Kept pedaling and falling until balance was mastered.

Happily rode all over creation.

The process was radically different for my oldest son, Graham. By the time he was three, he was doing something I never would have imagined was possible—learning to ride a bike without training wheels.

If you have kids, you're likely no stranger to this wonderful invention that allows for such a milestone to occur so early. But if you're not, what he's riding is called a balance bike. It's an interesting idea for helping kids learn to ride bikes. The old standard, training wheels, are based on the idea that kids need to learn to pedal before they learn to balance. When the wheels come off, the trick is to pick up the new skill of balancing on your bike.

With a balance bike, the end goal is still the same: give kids who can't ride a bike a way to exercise and learn the skills they'll need to ride a bike one day. The thing I like about the balance bike is that kids seem to be learning the tougher skill of balancing first. At first, Graham struggled, but he really did pick it up quickly—and from what I hear, his experience is pretty typical.

Before I knew about balance bikes, I would have thought a bike with training wheels was the only viable option for helping Graham learn to ride. It was the right scaffolding he would need to teach him to pedal, and then I'd run down the street behind him when we took the wheels off, much like my dad did for me, to help him learn to balance. But because someone rethought what it actually takes to learn to ride a bike, he was able to learn, and learn faster. Even better, I'm not sweating in the Texas sun as I run behind him.

Because I'm an especially nerdy guy, I can't see something like this and not make the connections to my work as an educator. It made me wonder if there are models to which we're holding too tightly in education. What are some long-held ideas that we could rethink? What would make your list?

Maybe it's grades. There's a lot of conversation out there on the ways we could rethink accepted practices with regard to student feedback. Perhaps it's your bell schedule. Is it serving students well or teachers well? Maybe it's the way you schedule students. What gets first priority—student needs or teacher preferences? Maybe it's the way you welcome new people to your building or to specific teams. Maybe it's the assumptions we make about student behavior. Or maybe it's the way we recognize professional development. Is there an effort to give individual teachers credit for time spent learning online?

Whatever the practice or idea, it's going to be unique to each campus. It's up to you to ask the questions about issues that need to be explored on your campus. Let's take some time to dig into a few of these topics.

# Grades: Should They Stay or Should They Go?

Stefano Salerno, an incredible educator I had the pleasure of teaching alongside and serving as an assistant principal, came to me one day with a question he had posed to his students: "If you had the choice for your next grade, would you choose an eighty-eight that you really worked hard for and learned something to earn, or ninety-five where you won't remember anything after the grade and didn't learn throughout the process?"

I love the question. Both the question itself and the thoughts I have about the implications of either choice fascinate me. Not surprisingly, many students opted for the ninety-five. They were sophomores in high school, and they were asked the question with just a few short weeks between them and their spring break, so I can understand the allure of some free points.

Still, there was much to discuss.

Salerno and I talked though his reactions and our mutual reactions to the students' choices while we watched a soccer game after school. I mentioned several articles and books on standards-based grading, dropping grades, and assessing for learning, and we continued talking for a while about our hopes for students and our desire for great learning to come from the feedback students receive from teachers. He mentioned that he wanted to follow up with these students, and I committed to touching base with him over the coming weeks.

A few days later, I stuck my head in just before the bell rang to begin class to ask if they'd had their conversation yet. I thought I would get a yes/no answer and maybe a quick recap as class started if they had talked. Instead, he invited me into his classroom and launched into a conversation about grades and learning. The students carried the conversation throughout the entire class period!

After hearing students share their responses to Salerno's initial question, the students seemed ready to press further into the conversation. I shared a few examples about how messy learning can be and how complicated that is to accommodate in a seven-period day for high school students. We went on to discuss the language that surrounds grading and considered what changes could look like in the system we are part of that still relies heavily on grades and GPA to allow students to open up opportunities for themselves after high school.

In the conversation about the language that surrounds grading, I really saw students begin to see the value in considering the impact grades have on their own learning. Many of the students, if they were honest, would probably admit they had responded out of convenience for themselves, initially with their teacher and even with me, when presented with the "struggle to learn for the eighty-eight or get the easy ninety-five and learn nothing" choice. They seemed to really understand the power of what was really at stake in considering the choice.

To be honest, they really impressed me.

I expected that they would come around eventually, but I didn't expect it to come so quickly. Students mentioned their desire to take tough classes as well as their reluctance to do so because of the fear of how lower grades might affect their GPA. They also mentioned the pressure to succeed (from themselves, their peers, their parents, their coaches). Two students asked pointed questions about how a no-grades classroom would work with eligibility for sports and extracurricular activities. Each of those questions has a variety of answers—although not all of those answers are viable, in my opinion. Then someone asked the question that has stuck with me the most: "Why don't teachers do this?" Why not, indeed.

> Students mentioned their desire to take tough classes as well as their reluctance to do so because of the fear of how lower grades might affect their GPA.

I was struck by the students' honesty that day as well as their enthusiasm for something that seemed so different from their normal, something that would daily ask more of them as learners. Our conversation also helped me see that the reasons students might be reluctant to change are similar to the reasons adults show reluctance when faced with new, potentially better, opportunities.

Grades have their issues, but the process is predictable and consistent. Though the game doesn't always measure what we'd like, students know and understand the rules. For teachers (and for me), I don't always love the idea of trying something entirely new when I know I'm going to be evaluated on it. Grades are established and safe. Shifting is risky.

## Daring to Tweak the Bell Schedule

A few years ago, while serving as an assistant principal at A&M Consolidated High School, my colleagues and I discovered something that many schools have stumbled upon: The students we wanted to come in for help before or after school were the least likely to do so. Whether it was circumstances outside of their control, involvement in extracurricular activities, or simple apathy, we weren't connecting with those students who needed extra help. It's not unique to our campus or even that out of the ordinary, but it was frustrating nonetheless.

As fate would have it, we noticed the need to do something different during one of the most significant changes our growing school district had come across in recent memory: the transition from one to two comprehensive high schools. At a time when our resources were on the cusp of being divided, what could we do to increase our ability to serve these students? We talked for weeks as a leadership team, trying to find something we could tweak, a detail we could change that would make a profound difference. It's an interesting process to go through. Trying to determine what makes the biggest difference to struggling students forces you to rethink many of your long-held assumptions about what really works in education.

We kept returning to the same basic idea: Teachers need more time with students to make a difference. Without that time, it's extremely difficult to make progress. Adding time to the school day was out of the question, so we were left searching for the next best option. Although I knew that the bell schedule is generally one of those sacred cows you just don't touch, I started tinkering with it. With the opening of the new high school, we would transition from serving 2,800 students to about 1,800 students. We were used to having four large lunches built into our fourth period over a two-hour time slot. I started to wonder to myself, "What if we served all our students in three lunches instead of four next year? What could we do with that other thirty minutes?" With four lunches, students had thirty minutes built into their day to catch up on homework, collaborate with their peers, or enjoy a bit of a brain break in the middle of the day. But that arrangement was far from ideal. Unless you had the same lunch as the teachers or students you needed to collaborate with, you couldn't take full advantage of the time. What if we effectively paused everything that was going on to provide a thirty-minute block of time for students to get the help they needed?

I finally convinced myself I had to share my idea, and I talked with a trusted colleague about the earliest draft of the plan. While I needed to refine my delivery, I left that conversation encouraged that I wasn't crazy for thinking my plan could actually work.

We ended up with a thirty-minute block of time from eleven o'clock to eleven thirty called Success Time. Students stayed put in their Success Time class with grade-level peers on Mondays for lessons on empathy, honesty, relationships, perseverance, and appreciating differences, and the rest of the week used that time for tutorials, class projects, or a brain break in the middle of the day. The shift even cleared up our hallways during the lunch hour and subsequently decreased referrals—because when students wander less, they make better choices. The positive changes didn't happen effortlessly, but they ended up being worth the effort.

Not every school needs to change its bell schedule, but for us it was a smart choice. Ultimately, rethinking what we often believe can't or shouldn't be touched is a great way to remember that it's best to put everything on the table when trying to imagine it better.

# Character in the Classroom

One of the things I miss most about the classroom is discussing novels with students and the way those stories helped students thoughtfully approach tough conversations. We'd open up *The Great Gatsby*, *Adventures of Huckleberry Finn*, or *Invisible Man* and dive headlong into some of life's biggest questions.

We'd talk about what it means to be valued as a person, walk through how easy it is to devalue people, and how hard it is to rebuild someone who has been made to feel unwanted or excluded. We'd spend time talking about the American Dream—what it meant to them, what it meant to the characters in the text, and whether it was still alive today. We'd invest in serious discussions about those who are invisible among us. We tackled countless issues and had thought-provoking conversations, but the best part was knowing I was equipping my students to engage their peers and their community for the better.

Though the basis for those conversations was literature, my students acquired a number of soft skills from that process—skills I believe are just as valuable as the exposure to a great novel. Over time, I noticed that my students were improving in four primary areas that would serve them well in the world. They were acquiring the following abilities:

### DISAGREE WITH AN IDEA INSTEAD OF A PERSON

Too often, we equate an opinion with an individual and miss out on a chance to learn something different. I think, as adults, we're pretty bad about this. We must get better at modeling this behavior in front of our students, and I think we can. This trait is powerful when it shows up. It allows for the open exchange of ideas, and people notice.

## REPAY WRONGDOING WITH KINDNESS

This idea goes against most of our cultural norms. In post-modern America, we have been taught that true success is having the most, being the best, and getting even when you've been wronged. Repaying a wrong with kindness is virtually unheard of, but I ask my boys to do this at home. They are three and five, and while I believe that consequences are important, I believe they are learning an important lesson about mercy, peacemaking, and restraint when I tell them to focus on their response rather than dwell on how each might have been wronged. What if more educators held themselves to this standard at school? I'm not asking anyone to get walked on, but think of all the opportunities you have during a single day to show students a better way. What an alternative to lashing out!

## SEE A SITUATION FROM ANOTHER PERSON'S PERSPECTIVE

I'm not big on ranking or creating a hierarchy of soft skills, but the ability to view any aspect of life from another person's perspective and let that inform your actions must be near the top. It's not an ability that can be forced, and it's rarely developed as quickly as we would like, but it is an absolute necessity to healthy relationships. Graduation requirements should be incomplete without some kind of class that explores this concept in detail.

## FIND HOPE, EVEN WHEN IT'S TOUGH TO SEE

I'm not asking you to be Pollyanna or look past a situation that calls for grief or sorrow. I do think it's valuable to train ourselves to find hope in situations where it might be obscured. Our brains like patterns, and everything I've seen and experienced indicates that positive patterns take more time to develop than their negative counterparts. So be intentional, find hope daily, and include your students in the search.

# The Questioner and the Doubter

I'm all for healthy discontent. I think it's helpful for us to brainstorm, rethink, and deliberate new ideas. That's how innovation happens. It's how creativity is sparked. But there's a striking difference between someone who is seeking to bring about positive change and someone who is simply being a curmudgeon.

Let me explain with an example from literature. In Cormac McCarthy's *The Sunset Limited*—an excellent play and well worth your time—two characters are engaged in a dialogue. The first mentions to the other, "I aint a doubter. But I am a questioner." The other responds skeptically saying, "What's the difference?" I love the way the first man replies: "Well, I think a questioner wants the truth. A doubter wants to be told there aint no such thing."

I love that distinction; questioners want the truth. The pursuit of a solution often gets lost in conversations doubters, though initially their critiques can look similar to a questioner's comments. The distinction is something we often fail to realize and, as a result, the hard work of many can be undone by a few dissenting doubters.

I believe it's the job of leaders to help push more people to become deeper questioners. Let's look at a few ways we can make sure we're on the right side of this distinction.

**A questioner is driven by wonder, but a doubter is blinded by limits.**

Ask more questions. Think about what could be. Consider the biggest obstacle, the one everyone knows about, the one everyone thinks can't change, and ask yourself what you would do if it were removed. Ask others what they might do. Then brainstorm some creative ways to work around the obstacle.

**A questioner knows he does not know; a doubter assumes he knows what can be known.**

Many doubters are stuck on the idea that they must have every last little thing figured out before moving forward. Some can't take a step without absolute certainty in their course of action. A questioner knows he does not know, and that sits okay with him. He's pursuing a solution, thirsty for an answer; but that doesn't cause him to dwell on the gaps in his current understanding.

**A questioner seeks greater understanding; a doubter discounts what he cannot understand.**

A questioner genuinely wants to know and understand more, and at times, it's not even for any purpose in particular. As a questioner pursues knowledge, he embraces struggle and acknowledges his limits. A doubter's faith lies within himself, and he fails to see the need to learn without a particular end in mind. That attitude narrows a doubter's perspective and prevents him from seeing a wide range of solutions to a problem.

All of the questioners I know believe there is great power in the collective. They know the value of sharing their knowledge, asking big questions, connecting to others, and listening carefully to others' ideas. They listen far more than they talk, and those with whom they interact end up rejuvenated and energized.

## When students leave your campus, what do they need to know to be successful, productive members of society?

---

These skills aren't cure-alls. They won't magically make everything better, but they're not a bad place to start. In my experience, students with these skills are better able to create peace, build bridges, show respect, and be thankful. If that's not worth pursuing, I don't know what is. So let's start imagining something a little better. What else do we need to instill in our students? When they leave your campus, what do they need to know to be successful, productive members of society?

# Professional Development

Another area I think is ripe for change is professional development. I vividly remember sitting in a large classroom where a lecturer was reading slides to us about how PowerPoint isn't a good way to help people learn. Seriously. It really happened. And yet, as laughable as that seems, I've been guilty of not doing much better when standing in front of our teachers.

When we get professional development wrong, we set up double standards, devalue the work that our teachers do to serve students as individuals, and lose credibility. When we imagine it better, we build credibility by doing the hard work of teaching in front of a group of educators who continually give their best to students.

In my first year serving as assistant principal at Cypress Grove Intermediate School, my principal and I knew we wanted our PD to challenge and support teachers on their self-selected goals for the year, and we also knew that we wanted staff to have time to implement some of the new things they learned about. More than that, we didn't want to talk at people for an extended period of time for professional development.

We decided to run the majority of our time as an Edcamp (with a bit of scaffolding). In a traditional Edcamp, participants design the day when they arrive to meet their needs with conversations among those who take part in the Edcamp. It's highly organic (which I really like), but it is a bit of an adjustment for many not familiar with the style of learning and a huge departure from the sit-and-get professional development many of us are trained to expect. To make sure our delivery didn't interfere with our message, we opted for the slightly more scripted version of the day.

To that end, we took the teachers' goals from the beginning of the year and teased out four common threads: student engagement, social emotional learning, growth mindset, and EdTech. With these in mind, we created a schedule for the day that allowed teachers to grow in their self-defined goals, but also pushed teachers to learn not simply with presentations, but primarily through conversations with each other about the topics at hand.

My favorite part about the whole experience was this: Before our time together, I got to talk with a huge number of the amazing educators on our campus, share the new crazy idea I had, and ask them if they would attend one of the conversations that we had planned for the day. I went on to explain that all they had to do was share the awesome ideas they are using in their classroom day in and day out. It felt absolutely incredible to get to tell so many folks that they would be an asset to this conversation. If we had awful weather and had to cancel the day of PD, it would have been worth it all to me just to have those affirming conversations with so many of the educators on our campus.

After the day, we got several thank yous; I don't share that to pat myself on the back. I share it because teachers enjoyed sharing with each other and embracing the struggle that comes with doing the hard work that educators are trusted to do each and every day. All I did was get out of the way. The entire day was about educators connecting with one another and realizing how much genius and awesomeness there is within our building just waiting to be shared. That's why it was worth it. That's why we'll do it again.

It was telling that I only received two pieces of feedback:

- When can we do this again?

- When we do this again, can we design part of the day that morning like a real Edcamp?

Absolutely. I think it's important to realize that all we did was pull an existing model into a new environment. We didn't invent this idea. We didn't reimagine anything or turn the world on its head. All we did was make a simple shift that had a big impact.

Teachers work too hard differentiating—trying new and risky tactics to engage students, and using their energy to do everything they can to reach students—for school leaders to sit back and offer the same kind of "teacher support" in the same way it has always been done. Whether you're a teacher or an administrator, we have to fight to do professional development differently—better. There is no time to waste.

In no uncertain terms, there is a lot to be reimagined in education. It's not limited to these topics, either. Educators are doing amazing things to imagine it better for students each and every day. In my own district, I see English teachers shifting from teaching whole-group novels to allowing students to self-select their major works. Huge shift, even bigger return on investment. I see teachers exploring giving students choice when it comes to the final products that demonstrate their mastery of new content and skills. I see teachers constantly questioning how to best engage their students, how to provide flexible seating to create welcoming learning environments, and how to truly teach the whole child. I see teachers engaged in vulnerable coaching conversations that would have been unimaginable for many just a few years ago. I see social emotional learning as a topic increasing in importance as we prepare students for the next challenges they will face—whether it's the next school or the next phase of life. I see administrators engaged in meaningful conversations about discipline and what we can do to truly help students learn how to respond differently the next time a similar situation presents itself.

I see teachers working through what it takes to really do project-based learning the right way and what it looks like to flip math classes so students get their work time with a teacher who can really help them as they struggle through the hard work of learning. I see all this, and I know I only see a fraction of what's out there. What change can you make? Where will you invest the time to imagine it better?

It's not an easy journey; don't try to go it alone. But find someone who's got a crazy idea like you and figure out how to imagine it better for you, your peers, and your students. You won't regret it.

# THRIVE
## SUMMARY QUESTIONS

What would you love to change about your classroom? Your school? Your professional life?

What do you want students to know that is not in your content standards?

List a few ideas for making that a reality.

List a few people who would be great at helping you out with this.

Revisit your reflections on "Teaching Expectations" and "Hook Your Students." What do you want to reimagine?

Write down your campus mission or vision statement. If you like it, how are you teaching those skills explicitly to students? If you don't like it, reimagine it and create a plan to teach students those skills.

What's the best professional development you've ever experienced?

How does that compare to the professional development you're used to receiving on your campus? In your district?

What will you do to make professional development different next time it's offered on your campus?

## CHAPTER 5

# Value Vulnerability

Vulnerability is the birthplace of innovation, creativity, and change.

—BRENÉ BROWN

## The **Myth** We Believe
The best teachers have all the answers.

## The **Truth** That Lets Us THRIVE
Vulnerability is prerequisite for all innovation, creativity, and change.

**I** *didn't always wear glasses.* In fact, if things had gone my way during that eye exam, I still wouldn't be wearing them. At fifteen years old, I knew I could pass my driving test, but I suspected I would have some trouble with the eye test required to get my permit. My vision wasn't terrible, but it wasn't that great, either. So in a moment of both panic and genius, while standing in line to get my eyes tested, I thought to myself, "Why not just memorize what the guy in front of me says?" I knew it was the perfect plan. Nobody would know I couldn't see and I wouldn't have to wear glasses. Feeling confident, I slid up to the machine, peered down into it while only halfway listening to the directions, and rattled off the letters I had memorized. But when I looked up, the instructor had the strangest look on her face. Thinking I must have set a record or done something equally impressive, I was blown away when she asked, "You can't tell those are numbers, can you?"

Not cool. In that moment, I was busted. Right there in my high school next to friends who had no problem passing the vision test, my weakness was exposed. Not only could I not see, I couldn't fake my way through the test. After multiple failures in a matter of moments, I confirmed I had an eye doctor, knew where the Department of Public Safety office was, and shrank back into my desk.

All because I was too scared and too proud to get glasses.

## Dealing with Your Limits

I hate it when I can't do something, and I don't think I'm alone. It's only natural to want to be strong and successful and knock it out of the park on the first swing. But that's not how life works. Too many of us forget that any kind of success, innovation, progress, or win often has to follow failure.

We praise innovation, creativity, resilience, risk, and grit, but we spend a surprisingly small amount of time talking about what it's like to publicly overcome failure as educators, with our weakness exposed and our shortcomings made plain for all to see. And I think this oversight impacts nearly everything we do. We hide, afraid of being known, afraid of not measuring up, and give off a nice, everything-is-okay vibe. But what if the solution is being honest about our faults and our blunders? What if the very thing we need is failure?

When I come across one of those moments where the mirror is held up and I see the gaps that exist between who I am and who I want to be, I'm forced in one of two directions: find a way to mask that gap and pretend it doesn't exist, or step into the reality of the gap and work through it with a little vulnerability. Neither one is a lot of fun, and I fail to make the right choice all of the time. But in those moments where I choose to call out my weakness and work through it with friends I trust, I find myself growing exponentially faster into the person I want to be.

There's a lot of buzz in education right now about vulnerability. Many are talking about how it impacts leaders and their ability to connect with others, and more are talking about the trust that would be required for school-wide risk taking to become a reality. If you ask me, we're starting the right conversations.

One of my favorite thoughts on this idea of vulnerability comes from author and researcher Brené Brown. From her perspective, "Vulnerability is the birthplace of innovation, creativity, and change." Hers is a pretty bold claim. Think about what's really at stake in that thought. She's saying that three of those things that seem nonnegotiable for student success—innovation, creativity, and change—are an impossibility without embracing vulnerability.

My worry is that when it comes to vulnerability, we're getting better at talking about it than at actually living it out. I've caught myself nodding along, agreeing that it would be great to take risks, and then realizing I don't know how that would even look at work. Resolving to be vulnerable in a professional setting is daunting, but wouldn't it be worth it to provide students with a learning experience defined by innovation, creativity, and change? Here are a few places I believe we can start:

## ADMIT YOU DON'T HAVE THE ANSWERS

As a teacher, I always wanted to appear as though I had it all together in front of my students. I worked hard to make sure I could answer any question that came my way about the literature we studied. I wanted students to be confident in my ability, and the result was that I almost exclusively operated out of the most secure place in the classroom. The problem is that the "I have it together" look deters students from taking a risk when they're not sure it's the right next step. Disrupting this tendency can be as simple as working new problems or writing a fresh first draft in front of our students instead of sharing previously prepared examples to show the potential missteps students might encounter during their work.

## ASK FOR CRITICISM

We all like to think we are open, available, and easy to talk to. Often though, I'm betting we give ourselves more benefit of the doubt here than we should. One way to show we are serious about making positive changes is to invite criticism. It shows we understand that real improvement involves having hard conversations. When asking others on campus for their feedback, I have found it's helpful to establish parameters to avoid comments that are overly general or overly specific. One option is to provide your colleagues with a questionnaire that includes two or three choices.

## TRY SOMETHING NEW

Pick out something new—maybe a short story, article, picture book, experiment, or math problem—and tackle it in front of your students as a first-time learner. Talk about it like most first-time learners would—with a little less polish, a little more guesswork, and the mistakes that come with learning something new displayed front and center. I think a lot of educators bury new ideas because they're not sure how to work through something that might fail. Trying something new and failing at it publicly can serve as a great model for other teachers who are struggling with the idea of taking on a specific challenge.

## OWN YOUR MISTAKES

Mistakes are inevitable. We must be willing to own them and use them as the point of departure for productive growth. In those times where we make tough decisions that impact others and things don't turn out well, I think it's important for others to hear us and see us take responsibility. That's not a popular narrative. For many, strength is all about covering up mistakes and appearing flawless and faultless. If we really want to foster the kind of campus culture that brings people together rather than pushing them apart, we have to be willing to take this sort of action at every level of leadership.

# The Role of Empathy

We talked earlier about the isolation that is common to educators. People are in and out of your classroom all day long. Your fellow teachers stand next to you in the hallways before school and after school. But for all the togetherness that each day brings, teachers spend an inordinate amount of time as the lone adult in a room with students. While I won't assume this was every educator's experience, I often compared myself to those around me and on the toughest days, I felt pretty beat up.

Brené Brown claims in *Daring Greatly*, "If we can share our story with someone who responds with empathy and understanding, shame can't survive." This is where our vulnerability transforms into an opportunity for exponential growth. Being vulnerable with your colleagues is not just talking about whatever is going on in your life; it's about being a person who is willing to step into the struggle with someone else and walk with them toward a better place. It's about being in the arena with them. It's about preparing to do incredible things alongside them. It's about them knowing that they are not alone in the challenging work before you both.

I can remember so many times when my colleagues showed me empathy when they didn't have to. It made a profound impact on me. The isolating nature of teaching only magnified my need for an empathetic response to my struggles. But as much as I can see the need for this type of response in me, I don't often go out of my way to look for situations where people might need the same. With that in mind, I present to you three common opportunities to extend empathy to those teaching in your hallway.

## THE OUT-OF-CONTROL-CLASS MOMENT

We associate a quiet classroom with a quality teacher, and when things get loud, it's really easy for us to compare our experience to that of another teacher. We begin to think, "Well, if you just did X, that wouldn't have happened." It's important to remember that even in those moments where that fix might be helpful in the long haul, we don't need to lead with fixing. We must first care for the person who just lived through that experience, and an empathetic response is a great place to start.

## THE EXHAUSTED-BUT-STILL-GOING MOMENT

Most teachers know what it's like to smile through exhaustion, keeping their distress quiet. I think we need to make it okay for rookies and veterans alike to speak honestly with each other about schedules, workload, and the physical and mental toll of teaching. I don't think we can underestimate the power of making sure others know that they're not alone in feeling overwhelmed.

## THE I'VE-DONE-EVERYTHING-AND-IT'S-NOT-WORKING MOMENT

We've all seen this happen. Your coworker planned everything diligently, factoring in a wide range of student interests and abilities. With painstaking care, she reworked a past lesson to help a few specific learners in one specific class. And it tanked. In that moment, some would be tempted to decide that teacher simply didn't do enough. But that teacher doesn't need judgment. She needs empathy, understanding, and time to vent.

# Getting Found Out

Thinking back on my driving test, it was absolutely imperative that I was found out. It would have been terrible, possibly even tragic, for everyone if I had faked my way through that eye exam. In that case, being exposed was for the best.

Since then, I've come to realize that being found out isn't such a bad thing. For all the things we agree on as educators, this seems like it should top the list. It's hard to be unsure about something. It's scary to act when you know you might not have all the answers. To be clear, I'm not asking you to do something that will put your job at risk, or cause you humiliation, or ruin your reputation. What I do think would benefit us all is to be honest about our uncertainty and talk about it publicly. We're all unsure about something, and it gets easier to bear when we let ourselves be unsure about it together. And together, we can work through those challenges more effectively than we can alone.

Not only is there far too much on the line for us to blink past the necessity of living vulnerable lives in our schools, there is so much of an upside in taking on even one of these challenges. Dismissing the idea of vulnerability altogether is a recipe for stagnation and regression.

It won't always be fun, but the work to open yourself to others, regardless of your role on campus, makes you a leader.

# No Whispers

I'm a big baseball fan. I love the rituals, the unwritten rules that you'd better not break, the history of it all, and James Earl Jones' speech about the sport in *Field of Dreams*. All of it. Baseball fans are an irrationally loyal bunch. When the Astros lost more than 100 games three years in a row, I still wore my gear. I even wore it more proudly. Because they're my team, and no matter how the season is going, I'm going to support my team.

One of my favorite baseball stories comes from the night before Robinson Cano returned to New York to play against his former team. Jimmy Fallon decided to help Cano get used to the boos he would experience at Yankee Stadium by setting up a huge cardboard cutout of Cano and letting New Yorkers boo at him. You know, to practice for their booing the next evening.

Except this was no ordinary cardboard cutout. Behind a curtain, Robinson Cano was waiting to meet the fans who were booing him. The fans did not disappoint, and hilarity ensued. At just the right moment, someone cued Cano to step forward as the boos came to a crescendo. You would expect a bit of shock from them. While that was part of their reaction, the more remarkable change came from their nearly instant switch from persistent booing to genuine gratitude for all he had done for their team and well wishes for him.

I love the reaction that people had when they realized he was there. How quickly they flipped from booing to embracing Cano, some of them literally hugging him! Nobody thought anything of these people yelling at a cardboard image of Robinson Cano because that reaction was expected. But when Cano showed up, they changed their language and their stance.

What if we chose to speak about people only in that positive light at school? Think about the power there. What conversations could you commit to starting? What conversations could you commit to ending? What if we assumed the best about each other and always extended the benefit of the doubt? What if we decided that we weren't going to allow others to talk poorly of students or colleagues? What if we only engaged in conversation that brought people together instead of dividing them into parts?

Think about specific conversations that you are part of at your school. What if those went differently? What if visitors entered and left your campus knowing that they mattered? What if families knew they were invited to participate in a culture of trust with their student on campus? What if you knew they weren't whispering about you? What if there were no whispers on your campus? What will we miss out on if we don't? And who will we hurt in the process?

If we value vulnerability and commit to responding to others with empathy, we must operate with no whispers on campus.

# THRIVE
## SUMMARY QUESTIONS

In what areas is fear driving your decision making?

Who can you ask for honest feedback about where fear might be driving your decision making?

Where do you see those you lead (students, teachers, administrators, parents, etc.) struggling to innovate and create change?

How can you step into a vulnerable space with them and model the risk taking that could lead to change?

What would you try if you knew you could not fail?

Write down a few changes you are trying to make right now. How is it going?

What is safe about it?

What is risky about it?

Who is helping you out?

What whispers need to be shut down on your campus?

What are the steps that you can take to help in that process?

Write out a timeline for putting this change into practice.

Tell someone about it who will hold you to it. My person is:

_____

CHAPTER 6

# Everyday Every Day

Legacy is not built in one day, but every day.

—GEORGE COUROS

## The **Myth** We Believe
The best educators earn respect with grand gestures.

## The **Truth** That Lets Us THRIVE
Everyday interactions are the relational foundation that much of our work rests upon.

**I've always wanted to be** one of those administrators who really connects with students. But as an introvert, instant rapport rarely happens naturally for me. That's not an excuse, it's just part of my reality. I have to fight against it. My inclination is to find a place where I can work and get things taken care of.

As we rolled over to a new year, I knew I wanted to stretch myself in this particular area. After dismissing all of the reasons why it might be a tough goal to achieve, I decided I wanted to take a selfie with a student every day that I'm on campus this semester. Keep in mind I also told myself I would do this the previous semester and utterly failed. A handful of selfies, maybe. No consistency, minimal impact, and public failure. Not what I like.

I knew this time needed to be different. There's just too much good that comes from those everyday interactions with students to miss this, especially if the biggest issue might be my comfort zone. The first thing I did was make an image to drop into our daily announcements that would ask students to come find me if they met the criteria.

Because I'm super cool and made a point to see *Rogue One: A Star Wars Story* more than once before the spring semester began, I figured it would be fun to connect with other students who had done the same.

Not surprisingly, quite a few sixth graders had seen the movie multiple times. Before taking the selfie, we nerded out in my office—because that's where my *Star Wars* toys are, naturally—and talked about how we liked the new movie, how awesome the end was, and how we shouldn't spoil it for anyone else. The next day, I wore my shirt the school band had given me and looked for a student who was wearing the same shirt. We took a selfie in our matching shirts. It was great.

It turns out I unintentionally created an environment where students are more interested in the daily announcements than ever before. They're asking to see them so they can see the selfie of the day and see if they fit the description. The most exciting part is having students come to see me every day to share things we have in common. It. Is. Awesome.

It doesn't cost me a thing, students are reaching out, and we are creating connections. It's also a great way to model appropriate social media behavior for these fifth and sixth graders who are eagerly looking for cues about how to interact on that platform. It's an everyday thing. Nothing too exciting. Just a selfie. Except it's not just a selfie. It's a connection. It's valuing something they value and like about themselves that they are willing to share with the assistant principal. We don't have to offer some grand gesture to students to make our interactions memorable and meaningful. That's what kids deserve. To be valued. To be loved. To be known.

As of this writing, students liked being on Instagram. That'll change, but those needs—to be valued, loved, and known—won't change. That's why we have to be about these everyday interactions every single day. Because every day we miss, we miss the opportunity to value, know, and love our kids.

## How Can I Connect?

As an assistant principal, I spend a lot of time in our hallways. At the very least, I'm there before school, during every passing period, in the cafeteria at lunch, and at parent pick-up after school. (Okay, I'm expanding to include some of our common areas, but work with me here.) Part of my job in each of those locations is to look for any issues—moments when students aren't meeting campus expectations—and while this is important, it's not exactly the sort of life-giving work I dreamed of doing when I grew up.

Over time, I began to wonder how I could use this time differently. I needed to accomplish the initial goal, but I wondered if I could repurpose or reframe my time in the hallways to make it about more than just enforcing expectations. I'm one who believes there's great value in initiating positive interactions with students, and it always frustrated me when I felt like all I did during a passing period was remind students to be on time, wear their IDs, and enforce the dress code.

Some of these ideas have been easier fits than others, but I've tried each one. Because so many educators are required to be visible in the hallways of their schools, I wanted to share these. I hope they will encourage you to take every opportunity to value, love, and get to know your students!

# Five Positive Hallway Conversations

1) **Address a student by name during each passing period.** I'm not great with names. At the beginning of each year, I know a lot of names, and I know even more faces. They slowly match back up throughout the year. Using students' names in the hallway helps me continually increase the number of names I can easily recall. If you see someone you know, ask that student how the day is going. If you don't see anyone you know, learn a new name. Students often walk the same routes. Get to know them as they move past your location in the building.

2) **Hold a door open for students.** One afternoon I held the door open for some students as they walked toward our parent pick-up area. It created a natural conversation space for me to interact with students, and some positive conversation came out of it that wouldn't have

# I wondered if I could repurpose or reframe my time in the hallways to make it about more than just enforcing expectations.

otherwise. Students often have the perception that my primary duty is correcting their mistakes. While that's certainly one of my responsibilities, it's far from my entire job. Holding open the door puts me in a place of service to students. I like that.

**3) Wish students good luck when they compete.** When I worked at A&M Consolidated, we had close to 500 freshmen on campus, and seeing the volleyball, football, and cross country athletes in their respective gear at the beginning of the year helped me learn several names during time in the hallways. The list expands when including all the students who excel in academic competitions and fine arts performances. Obviously, we should talk to kids about more than their involvement in extracurricular activities, but wishing students luck on something they care deeply about is a great way to spark conversations.

**4) Recognize students for meeting expectations.** Some people find this odd, but I'm a big believer in providing positive reinforcement to all students who choose to meet expectations. In a seven-period day, students could encounter nine different sets of expectations—in the cafeteria, in the hallways, on the school bus—and getting it all right is no happy accident. Rewarding students with a bit of acknowledgment shows them we are noticing their efforts to do things the right way. I think that matters.

**5) Ask a consistent question and notice when you get an irregular response.** For me, this revolves around student IDs. Our students are expected to wear their school IDs when on campus, much to the chagrin of some, but everyone slips up from time to time. I regularly ask the same basic question, "Do you mind putting on your ID for me?"

It's not the most direct way to communicate the wear-your-ID message. And a student could certainly refuse, but I'm good with that. You see, what students see as a simple question about a campus expectation, I use for much more. I'm constantly looking for students who might not react appropriately so I can intervene and figure out what's going on. Maybe life got turned upside down since school ended the day before. Maybe something is going on between this student and another. Maybe the student missed breakfast for some reason. Asking a consistent question helps me intervene when bigger issues may be at play. It has a fringe benefit of identifying students who might need some coaching as to how to address adults appropriately. Either way, it's informing my next steps, which I like.

*I hope this list will be useful to you, but remember that your interaction with students doesn't have to be elaborate or meticulously planned. It does need to be genuine and heartfelt. Here are a few more ideas about making the most of the everyday I want to share—not because I have it all figured out or even because you haven't heard them before—but because I know I need to be reminded of these things myself.*

## Asking a consistent question helps me intervene when bigger issues may be at play.

# Invest Time in Relationships

As teachers, we are responsible for meeting our students' academic needs. It's our responsibility to make students feel welcome in class and create an environment in which they know there are consequences for failing to meet academic and behavioral expectations. We must also make sure they know one of those consequences is that we're going to pick ourselves up and keep learning.

## Listen Without Judgment

As a high school English teacher, I had many opportunities to explain ideas in an official capacity. As the teacher, the onus was on me to answer questions like, "What did the author mean when he did X?" or "What's the author saying about the state of society today when her characters respond like that?" Rather than answering those questions myself, I tried to model the struggle the authors were often encouraging readers to grapple with and pushed the responsibility for answering the question out to the students. At that point, my role shifted from question answerer to conversation facilitator, which I greatly preferred. Students were free to sort through their beliefs as we explored the narratives we encountered. It was interesting to see those who had seemed so sure of themselves get stuck when they paused to carefully consider the implications of their positions. But most often I was floored by the quiet students who used the opportunity to share their brilliance with the class. This doesn't happen if we're giving them the answers.

## Extend Grace

I'm a firm believer that students benefit from high expectations. But more than sending out individuals capable of meeting and exceeding the highest expectations from life's next challenges, I hope we produce young people who are ready to make the humane decision when the time calls for it. Learning doesn't happen in a linear fashion for most students. I certainly can't draw a linear timeline to tie many of my own learning experiences together. And yet so often, I get the feeling that teachers feel they don't have permission to yield to their better judgment and extend grace to a student. I don't mean to say that we have armies of teachers out there waiting to enforce rules simply because they are the rules, but I don't think we can do any harm by taking the pressure off some of our students. Extending grace to students dealing with extenuating circumstances makes a huge impact.

## Notice When It's an Off Day

Students rarely enter the room and announce that their day isn't going well. At least not in as many words, right? The effects of an off day show up in all sorts of other forms. Maybe a student takes out anger on you instead of the source of frustration, or maybe a student shuts down and refuses to put effort into his or her academic work. Identifying those common off-day characteristics is important, as is considering how we respond when we notice it. One day I came back from being out, and a student in my first period told me this: "Mr. Hogan, I was having a bad day, but you weren't here. You always seem to notice it and make those days better." As a fairly introverted teacher, I was just looking for things I could make conversation about. I had no idea the impact I was having. I'll never forget that.

## Admit Your Failures

Somehow part of being a leader has morphed into presenting yourself as flawless. I can't stand that. The reality is that we all are making plenty of mistakes. Not careless ones—just regular, everyday accidental mistakes. If we don't show our students a model for taking ownership of our mistakes, what are we saying to them about how they should handle their own? It's important in all contexts, but it's a special priority of mine to make sure young men see grown men own up to their missteps—whether big or small—and respond appropriately. Many teachers do a great job of this, but the impact is only increased as more educators step into that place of vulnerability. It's not always fun, but it's always worth it.

Stepping up to any of these challenges will likely make your job more complicated, but it can also make it more rewarding. Your impact as an educator doesn't happen by accident. I'm constantly looking for ways to improve in this area, and curating a working list of connections I can make with students helps me make sure that I make this goal a reality. Check it out below and think about what you might add to your own list.

## The Big List of Ways to Create Awesome Connections and Shared Experiences with Students

### THINGS TO DO

- Offer a high five, fist bump, or selfie.
- Plan out some random acts of kindness.
- Open a door for students.
- Help clean up a mess.
- Pass out "You are awesome" notes during passing periods.
- Address students by name.
- Go learn a student's name that you don't know already.
- Find time to visit a student's event (a game, a concert, a performance, whatever they value).
- Look for what they put on their backpack or what shirts they wear and find ways to make connections using that info.
- Drop in on an after-school game or club meeting and spend time with students doing what they love.
- Find a little time to go play with students during recess or P.E.
- Speak a greeting to each student who comes across your path.
- Visit students' classrooms and show an interest in their work.
- Attend a student performance after school.
- Complete a writing assignment that students are assigned and ask if you can share it on presentation day. If this scares you, make sure that you do it. It'll make a huge impact.

# Belonging Precedes Believing

It's true for students. True for teachers. True for nearly everyone in our schools. They want to feel like they are part of something, and the way we include or exclude people deeply impacts their initial perceptions of our efforts to help them. And this isn't just wrapped up in what we say. It's in the way we greet people. The way our campuses look at first sight. What people see when they drive by the bus loop and parent pick-up.

It's our duty to include others each and every day at school because before they will believe we mean what we say, they need to feel like they belong to the larger community. That sense of belonging is what leads people to trust educators when we say ...

- We put kids first.

- We do what's best for all students.

- We're a family here.

In our work at school, belonging precedes believing.

# THINGS TO TALK ABOUT

- The latest movies
- The school's next big game
- The school's most recent win or loss
- An amazing book
- How you spent your weekend
- Favorite TV shows
- Favorite sports teams
- Big plans for the upcoming weekend
- Fun road trips or other vacations
- Growing up in the community where you teach
- How the day is going
- How the student's last game went
- Their plans for the weekend (***Pro tip:*** Always give students an out. Ask, "Do you have any big plans for the weekend, or are you just going to chill?" so that students who don't have big plans (or the means to have big plans) don't feel excluded in your conversation.
- What they think you have in common with them
- What work he or she is proud of from this year
- What students are learning in class that day
- Where students have seen growth in themselves since last year
- What students want to accomplish by the end of the month/semester/year
- Who their favorite teacher is
- Ask them to go tell that teacher what makes them their favorite!

- What they think makes your campus great
- What they look forward to most at school
- What they would change if they were in charge for a day
- What advice they wish they could go back and give a younger version of themselves
- What they wish people knew about them
- A talent they wish they had (then figure out a way to help them start to develop that one!)

# THINGS WORTH NOTICING

- When students are meeting dress code (especially during those peak times when many aren't)
- When students are getting to class on time
- When students show kindness to a student they don't know
- When students listen to another student in need
- When students take time to show empathy to others
- When students go out of their way to perform random acts of kindness
- When students are wearing their ID like they are supposed to
- When students leave their lunch table cleaner than they found it.
- When students go out of their way to make sure all students have people to sit with at lunch

# THRIVE
## SUMMARY QUESTIONS

Everyday interactions are the foundation of campus culture. What are some small, everyday things that can ruin classroom or campus culture?

When these show up in your classroom or on your campus, how do you counteract them?

How can you tell when students have meaningful relationships with their teachers?

What are those little things that make the difference?

## SHATTERING THE PERFECT TEACHER MYTH

Make a list of the people whose everyday interactions make your day better at work.

List some ways you could thank them in a meaningful way.

List some specific times during your school day when you want to be deliberate about pursuing everyday interactions.

Who are some of the people you will look for? Take a minute to put these reminders on your calendar.

CHAPTER 7

# Inviting Others to THRIVE

I love the man that can smile in trouble, that can
gather strength from distress, and grow brave
by reflection.

— THOMAS PAINE

**I'll be the first to admit** that, even with the best of intentions, I've read plenty of books, nodded along with the good ideas inside, and gone back to my busy life without making many changes. There's too much on the line for that to happen here. That's why this book is an invitation to a journey, the start of a quest.

Where are we going? We are headed away from a place of isolation and into a world where we are sharing fantastic ideas with others in a way that inspires them to make changes. Think of the good that will come from just a few conversations. Students will be empowered. Teachers will feel satisfied with their work. The snowball will continue to grow as it moves in the right direction.

You have countless experiences that are inspiring you and your colleagues to do great things in your classrooms and on your campuses each day. If we don't spend time reflecting on those experiences, we risk losing not only the momentum that builds when things are going right, but also the lessons we are learning along the way.

John Dewey said, "We do not learn from experience. We learn from reflecting on experience." Read that carefully. We do not learn from experience. That's counterintuitive to nearly everything I had heard before I first came across Dewey's claim, but I believe what he's saying. I also believe it has become nonnegotiable. If we want to thrive, we must be committed to learning through reflection.

I want to take it a step further, though. I want you to not only reflect, but also to share those reflections with others in your field. I want you to blog. I want others to learn from you. I want the world to be better because you have added your genius to it.

I'm not a mind reader, but I suspect that many of you, right at this moment, are coming up with reasons this is a terrible idea. Chief among them are these two questions:

*What do I have to say?*

*When will I have time to blog?*

These aren't the only concerns, but they are probably the most common. They were two big concerns for me when I started blogging, but the good news is that throughout this book I've been equipping you to overcome these obstacles. Educators who want to thrive are committed to their own professional growth and to that of others. There's no reason that time and confidence should stand in the way.

## Choosing a Topic

If you've been writing on all the mostly-blank pages in this book, you've already taken the first step on your journey toward becoming a blogger. The best place to start is to write about what you already know.

Here are a few prompts to get you started.

## TEACHING EXPECTATIONS

- Why students need to be taught behavior expectations, not just told them
- How to isolate behaviors that need to be retaught and even thought through
- How visitors to your campus might react to the behaviors that are common on your campus
- How to identify and encourage teachers who excel at teaching behavior expectations

## HOOK YOUR STUDENTS

- Write about why compliance isn't (and can't be) our goal. Engagement outweighs compliance.
- Discuss ways that personal passions could be leveraged into meaningful connections with students.
- Talk about ways to support a developing teacher as he or she works through the early years as a teacher.

## REJECT ISOLATION

- Isolation stagnates growth. Connections cultivate it.
- Write about a professional connection you've made and how you plan to maintain that relationship.
- Examine why some educators are likely to end up isolated on your campus and what role you can play in preventing that isolation.

## IMAGINE IT BETTER

- The status quo need not be protected. Let's imagine school better for our students.

- What do you want students to know past your curriculum?
- Share the ways you experience learning through professional development and how you can be part of creating great professional development on your campus.

## VALUE VULNERABILITY

- Vulnerability is not weakness, but a source of strength.
- In what areas can you help create safe space for your peers to be vulnerable?
- What aspects of your professional life are you trying to change right now?

## EVERYDAY EVERY DAY

- Everyday connections create the lasting impressions that change students' lives.
- Share conversation starters that will create connections with students.
- Specific times throughout the day that you can purposefully connect with students

# THAT'S AMAZING!

I know what you're thinking. There's a good chance you've already given in to that voice that says, "But people have already heard about that topic; I don't need to write on it!" You're not alone thinking this, but we have to work together to shake off this confidence-destructor and get our ideas out there! We have to quiet that voice. I dare you to watch "Obvious to You. Amazing to Others" by Derek Sivers and believe that you have something valuable to share.

## We have to get our ideas out there!

# Find Your Voice

I have found that the best topics to blog about are those topics that get you fired up. The ideas that excite you, scare you, annoy you, and drive you to do your best. When we delve into what we're passionate about, that passion attracts others, and it can inspire them to tackle their own challenges along the way.

Sometimes it helps to write about whatever comes to you. The next time you are casting about for topics, let your mind wander freely in regard to your profession. I have found it helpful to ask these questions, and I'm sure you can think of others:

- What's something new I've learned in the past month?
- What's something I am currently trying to master?
- What was my best day in school in the past few weeks, and why was it so encouraging?
- What was my worst day and what went wrong? What did I learn from it?
- What two things would I change in my classroom? Or on my campus?
- What's my response to a prevailing education trend?
- What's my response to a long-held education policy that's currently being challenged?
- What's something real and honest, whether it reflects failure or success, that I could share with other educators?

More than anything, write. You'll get better as you go, and the topics will continue to flow your direction.

# The Obstacle of Time

Educators who are doing their jobs know the reality of time constraints. Our days are filled with deadlines, and all sorts of things that seem out of our control appear to eat up our time. I get that nobody has extra time. At the time of this writing, I'm a husband, a dad to a five-year-old, three-year-old, and one-year-old, a member of a church, and an assistant principal to just over 1,000 fifth and sixth graders. I co-founded a weekly Twitter chat—#CSISDchat at 8 p.m. CST every Tuesday. I'm an avid buyer of books, and sometimes I even find time to read them. The reality is that I'm nowhere near as busy as some of you are. I still fail in this area all the time, and I'll never go so far as to say I understand your schedule, the demands on your time, or all the details of your life. I don't. What I can say is these three practices have helped me radically improve my ability to carve out time to blog.

### 1) Keep a working list of ideas.

Keep a notebook of ideas so that you have plenty to choose from when it's time to sit down and write. Nobody has time to waste, so you'll want to be able to maximize your efforts.

### 2) Don't get bogged down in editing.

Hitting the "publish" button is still an adrenaline rush for me. It's exciting to put ideas out there, but it's not something that happens without a little bit of fear creeping in, too. My advice? Don't spend too much time editing. Edit for clarity and typos, but once you've said what you have to say, get it out there. I'm a write-it-skim-it-share-it kind of guy.

### 3) Schedule time to blog.

We'd all like to have endless pockets of free time pop up on our schedules. That's not reality. You're a busy educator doing everything you can to serve others. You're going to have to put it on your calendar. Literally. Write it down on a specific day and treat it as seriously as a parent conference. You wouldn't skip that, would you? If blogging is reflection, and reflection is how we learn, you owe it to yourself to set and maintain this meeting with yourself.

# What Happens When You Blog

*It is not the critic who counts; not the man who points out how the strong man stumbles, or where the doer of deeds could have done them better. The credit belongs to the man who is actually in the arena, whose face is marred by dust and sweat and blood; who strives valiantly; who errs, who comes short again and again, because there is no effort without error and shortcoming; but who does actually strive to do the deeds; who knows great enthusiasms, the great devotions; who spends himself in a worthy cause; who at the best knows in the end the triumph of high achievement, and who at the worst, if he fails, at least fails while daring greatly, so that his place shall never be with those cold and timid souls who neither know victory nor defeat.*

*—Theodore Roosevelt*

Blogging has a certain number of unpredictable factors attached to it, but there are a few things you are likely to encounter when you start to share your learning online. I'd like to highlight a few just to make sure you're prepared.

## CRITICISM FROM TROLLS

The Internet is a wonderful place. Everyone has an opinion, and in their unabashed attempts to share their ideas with others, some will try to lay waste to your thoughts. Internet trolls are a real thing. The good news is that all of the social media I can think of allow you to block someone. Do so. Do it liberally. We've already talked about how little time we have and about how valuable that slight margin is. Don't give your attention to people who aren't about what you're about. As Roosevelt says, "It is not the critic who counts. … The credit belongs to the man who is actually in the arena." Anyone can crash your party. It takes guts to share, and you have them!

# CONSTRUCTIVE CRITICISM

Unlike the previously mentioned criticism, this is feedback that pushes you to refine your ideas, rethink your assumptions, and clarify your claims. It happens when thoughtful educators come across your excellent ideas. It will happen sooner than you realize. Be careful not to confuse the two forms of criticism. Every now and then one of those trolls approaches as a wolf in sheep's clothing. When authentic and well-meaning pushback comes, embrace the conversation and learn from the exchange.

# NOTHING AT ALL

The total lack of response after posting a blog used to bother me. I'd spend time writing a blog post, my whole write-it-skim-it-share-it routine, and nothing would happen. Nobody would read it. No trolls. No educators who might agree or push back. Nothing. As a result, I learned an important lesson: If you blog with the express purpose of scoring readers, you will end up disappointed. If you are blogging with the desire to share what you're learning or what you're struggling with, other educators will find it. Sometimes it just takes a while. Don't lose heart; keep writing.

# SUPPORTERS AND CHAMPIONS

You posted your blog, and it was one that gave you a few butterflies before you put it out there. Then the most amazing thing happened. Someone reads about your struggle, and offers those all-important words, "Me too." Just like that, the doubt about sharing vanishes. I can't wait for you to experience that moment. When you realize you aren't alone, it's easier to fight the feeling that sharing your learning isn't having an impact. Soon enough someone will come along and share that they had thought about something similar for a while, but had never thought they could pull it off. You might laugh now and think that it will never happen, but it will. And when it does, it'll fill your tank for at least a couple of weeks. Your work is valuable, and your efforts to share your learning and your experiences through your blog are going to have a substantial impact on more than you know.

## OTHERS WILL SPRINGBOARD OFF OF YOUR IDEAS TO ACCOMPLISH EVEN GREATER THINGS

Remember that rock-star team of teachers I mentioned a while back who helped me start my career in education? We functioned this way. One would share an idea, and though the idea was solid, the springboard it provided was the real gift. Amazing things came out of those conversations, and I was floored the first time a parallel experience surfaced through an interaction on my blog.

As you share your learning, you'll propel others toward greatness. In that, you'll become the kind of leader who inspires others to learn and grow and do more.

When you blog, your confidence will grow. When your confidence grows, writing will become easier. When the writing becomes a little easier, you'll write more. And when you write more, your writing will be filled with increased confidence, more fluid writing, and that feeling that your writing is out there making a difference. (It's not just a feeling. It *is* making a difference.) So get to writing and start sharing!

# Blogging: 3 Things Not to Do

1. Don't use student names or identifying characteristics. Family Educational Rights and Privacy Act (FERPA) guidelines and general privacy standards are a real thing. You have much to offer. Don't taint the process with this serious misstep.

2. Don't use your blog as a place to complain. That's happening in a workroom near you (avoid it), and you're a person who has solutions. Offering critiques and posing solutions are not the same as griping.

3. Don't write something you don't want connected to your name. Forever. It's OK to write a reflection and not post it. If you don't want it on the front page of the paper next to your name, don't post it.

# THRIVE
## SUMMARY QUESTIONS

Write down five blog topics you feel you could write today.

1.

2.

3.

4.

5.

Where will you keep your notebook of ideas?

When will you carve out time to blog? Write down three potential times here:

1.

2.

3.

Write down your fears about sharing your learning. Come back to this in two months.

Craft a blog post about how you are working through these obstacles. Be sure to put a reminder in your phone to check back here.

Find an inspirational blog post that you really love and write about how you are going to live out the charge the author set forth. Commit to sharing the first post and your response with at least one teacher you work with daily.

If you come across a blog post with a claim that rubs you the wrong way, consider writing a rebuttal. Don't write a complaint, but a thoughtful criticism of your concerns and what you would do differently is a helpful way to process your own views.

CHAPTER 8

# Working with Survivors

The only way to do great work is to love what
you do. If you haven't found it yet, keep looking.
Don't settle.

—STEVE JOBS

You probably know a few naysayers.
They specialize in being able to counter any great idea with
"Yeah, but..." before you've even finished presenting it. They
don't like to change, or grow, or learn. They are the great defenders of
the way that we've always done it, even if we don't know why that might
be the case, and it's hard to know how to respond to them at times.
If you're not careful, interactions with naysayers can rob you of your
excitement for creativity and change in education.

Maybe there aren't naysayers in every school, but I'm comfortable
claiming that they are in far more schools than they should be. That

means, we need a plan to deal with them, because the reality is that although educators start out wanting to thrive, passion and drive are easy to lose when faced with negativity. When that happens, something subtle, but significant, occurs to educators. Instead of being change agents doing all we can to thrive, those who give in to negativity and approach each day just to get by opt to simply survive. Those who want to thrive won't idly allow that to happen. We need a plan to counteract negative forces. But here's the thing about a plan, if we're going to attempt to turn folks around, we have to believe the best about them. We have to believe they can change.

> If we're going to attempt to turn folks around, we have to believe the best about them. We have to believe they can change.

I'd like to offer up five responses to the common objections raised by resident naysayers. My hope is that these responses will help guide you through difficult conversations about change on your campus.

*1) "Yeah, but we've always done it this way."*

You would be hard pressed to find a phrase that more clearly demonstrates a fixed mindset in an educator than this one. A lot of work has been done to clarify the ways students benefit from a growth mindset, but I assert we need to apply those same efforts to faculty. If you're a leader, find some time for teachers to pursue what could be, what might be, and what needs to be reviewed so that we can imagine it better. If you're a teacher, ask for that time to think through what you might be able to tinker with or redesign to better serve your students. Regardless of your title, think about ways you can help celebrate successes on your campus, especially when they result from trying something new that served students really well.

## 2) "Yeah, but I will have to work more."

Unfortunately, the path of least resistance is well worn for some. This statement is less likely to be communicated verbally and more likely to be seen in action. For that teacher who continually invests the bare minimum, a straightforward invitation to collaborate might be helpful. Make sure you ask for help on something that you know that teacher feels capable of tackling. Go out of your way to genuinely thank that person after the fact.

## 3) "Yeah, but it won't work because of a problem with part X."

Critical feedback, as long as it's not negativity for negativity's sake, can be a great filter for new ideas. Naysayers are at least thinking critically about the ideas that have been presented to them. One option is to ask the naysayers to help troubleshoot new ideas. If they are good at it, make it their job to find and suggest solutions to flaws. If they aren't great at troubleshooting, mentor them on how to make more meaningful contributions to their school community. Incorporating naysayers into the overall team process empowers them to have a profound impact rather than being someone who exists on the fringes.

## 4) "Yeah, but I don't benefit from that."

Drive the conversation back to your school's core values and purpose. Maybe that means literally passing out copies of a mission statement. Maybe it's a heartfelt story about student success or a list of alarming statistics about student demographics. Find an idea worth chasing and use it to refocus your efforts by reminding your colleagues of the ultimate goal.

## 5) "Yeah, but I don't want to get better."

Okay, most naysayers aren't actually going to say this out loud, but they manage to get the message across. Try to start a conversation about what you're learning. It might not even be something related to education. See if you can find common ground that relates to personal interests. Most people have something they enjoy that they'd like to get better at. That could be a place to start.

Gut Check: Be honest. Did you think, "Yeah, but ..." when I started discussing the need to adopt a new mindset when dealing with negative colleagues? If so, remember that. We all do it, and even with the best intentions, it's tough to change old habits. Doing so takes time and effort.

I hope that these ideas jump-start conversations of hope for you and your colleagues, but I know they are only a first step toward a new way of thinking. I believe, though, the growth they can bring over the long haul is well worth the initial discomfort. Teachers who are willing to take an active role in this process have the chance to redefine themselves as educators who are willing to thrive and help others do the same. Don't let others settle and become those who don't strive to thrive.

## It Better Be Real

I spent some time looking at cars a while back, and although I didn't end up with a new vehicle, I came away with this insight: Using a relationship to get something you want is garbage.

At one dealership, I worked with a salesman who was determined to go the relational route to make the sale. He did everything he could to fast-track our little relationship. Even before we really got started, he was taking care of me. "Do you need anything? What can I get you before we head out to the lot?"

With my ice-cold water in hand, we made our way to the vehicle. He asked if I had a family and about my kids before telling me about himself, and he asked what I was driving at the moment. As we got to the vehicle, he launched into the safety features and how they would protect my kids in the back seat in the event of an accident. He hopped into the car and we were off, but not before he asked what kind of music I liked so that he could tune the radio accordingly. After finding a station he thought would match my musical taste, he asked about our

# Most people have something they enjoy that they'd like to get better at. That could be a place to start.

purchase of a van at a large store in a bigger city down the road. "So, how was that?" he asked with more than a hint of judgment. After I explained the experience was fine for us, he chimed in, "But, it's just so impersonal there, right? You're just in, out, and that's it."

Feeling a little judged for my previous car-buying experience (which was just what we wanted), I decided to shut my mouth for a minute (an introvert trick some car salesmen don't know about, I think) and let him direct the conversation. He asked what my wife did for a living. Here's where things got complicated because I chose to answer his question the way I would if a friend were to ask. I proceeded to tell him about the work that the organization my wife worked for does to make the world a better place. It works to end child slavery in Ghana by helping villages learn to fish more efficiently using aquaculture in exchange for the freedom of the child slaves whom they then reintegrate into their families.

He seemed to get uneasy at this point, and I now wonder if it's because he just didn't know where to go next. You see, just like anyone else who has done this before, I know that there are really only four things he needs to know: my desired monthly payments, credit, downpayment plans, and trade-in, if any. He chose the pseudo-relational route to try to get this information. But the thing is, the people with whom I have relationships don't act like that. On one hand, our interactions looked like a relationship, but on the other, he was feigning interest and concern as a way to get close to me quickly so that he could make a sale.

That's his job, and maybe I was foolish to think anything else might happen on a trip to a car dealership, but the whole thing got me thinking about relationships in schools. Teachers are not salesmen, but sometimes, I'm afraid, we come off that way. In fact, some of our students know the drill and can see it coming better than I saw it at the car dealership. They know what to expect when an educator is trying to connect with them, and they know it's likely going to look like a relationship. Sometimes that's OK, but it's our responsibility to make sure we are being genuine with our students.

## If we're using relationships to accomplish other goals, we're in the wrong.

Let me be clear: I think authentic relationships are the key to any community's health, and I'm in no way advocating abandoning this sort of approach. What I do believe is that if we're using relationships to accomplish other goals, we're in the wrong.

The way we model relationships with all of our students has to be authentic to what we believe relationships should be. Survivors let this fall short. If you want to thrive, we can't miss the opportunity to connect with students relationally. Relationships matter because people matter—not because they have a particular fringe benefit that helps us accomplish some other goal. Using relationships to get a student to behave, to get a piece of information, or to do anything other than value another person—regardless of age, race, creed, orientation, or any other way you can categorize a person—means that we've missed the mark. Does that mean that teachers who have deeper relationships with their students don't often reap some of those benefits? No. Of course not. But that benefit is not the point.

I always found that students had a keen eye for the difference between the teachers who genuinely wanted to get to know them and those who knew that developing a relationship was a box to check, a passive part of their work that was expected of them, but not a priority.

Having a positive relationship with a student is different than simply knowing something about him. Teachers who just survive might learn a few facts about students in August, but teachers who THRIVE make getting to know their students a priority all year.

Starting with the next interaction we have, let's get it right. Get to know the folks on your campus because they're people and because that makes it worth it. That makes it real.

# THRIVE
## SUMMARY QUESTIONS

Think of an issue or change to which you strenuously objected, aloud or otherwise, that ultimately turned out well. How did you come to see it differently? What helped you the most?

What are some sacred cow issues you're holding on to?

What's a practice, event, or policy at your school that you don't want to see changed? If you examine the reasons, what do you come up with?

Before you move on to the rest of your day, think of one person who you can consider differently. Write down a name, and commit to growing yourself as you grow others.

CHAPTER 9

# When We're Not Enough

It is impossible to live without failing at
something, unless you live so cautiously that you
might as well not have lived at all—in which case,
you fail by default.

—J.K. ROWLING

In the book, *The Short and Tragic Life of Robert Peace*, Jeff
Hobbs tells the unforgettable true story of his college roommate,
Robert Peace. Aptly titled, Peace's story ends both tragically and all
too soon. Here's the summary from the back cover of advance copies
of Hobbs' book:

> *Robert Peace was born outside Newark, in a neighborhood
> known as "Illtown," to an unwed mother who worked long hours
> in a kitchen. Peace's intellectual brilliance and hard-won deter-
> mination earned him a full scholarship to Yale University. At col-
> lege, while majoring in molecular biophysics and biochemistry, he*

*straddled the world of academia and the world of the street, never revealing his full self in either place. Upon graduation from Yale, he went home to teach at the Catholic high school he'd attended, slid into the drug trade, and was brutally murdered at age thirty.*

For the longest time, I wrestled with that. How could his story end this way? Everything was in place, right? Robert Peace had what we've all been told it takes—determination, intelligence, supportive peers, professional connections—but it wasn't enough to keep his life from ending tragically. Countless people have succeeded with far fewer advantages than Peace had. How did he end like that?

That's what I can't understand; it's what leaves me frustrated. Because when we have everything in place, the plan is supposed to work. Our efforts should be enough. We should be enough, right?

## How Do We Respond?

When it feels like we're not enough, we have to remember that our efforts have their limits and that our students are the ones who must take final ownership over their decisions. We can want circumstances to change, we can set up opportunities to make change accessible for students, and we can stress the importance of taking advantage of the opportunities set before them. However, we cannot make the choice for students. On more than one occasion, this has left me feeling like a failure after a student didn't take the path we laid out for them.

I hate that feeling of failure. Because it's not just about me; it's about decisions that will forever shape a student's future.

For a while, it was convenient to believe that everything teachers do—providing choices, developing meaningful relationships, and helping bridge racial, gender, and socioeconomic gaps—was so compelling that students couldn't resist it. Many times, it would take extending only one or two of these olive branches to create a positive change, and in tough situations, the right one-two combination always seemed to make the magic happen. You just had to get to know the student, prove you were in it for the long haul, and meet the needs that were there (and the process seemed to work even more smoothly if you helped determine those through your own relationship with a student).

Don't get me wrong; I don't mean to sound flippant. Serving students this way is what I always loved doing. I would go as far as to say I felt called to this profession, even designed to do this. And in many cases, I felt like I did this well.

Then there's Robert Peace's story. His situation isn't perfect, but his story sure starts out looking like a movie script for the student who is going to overcome the odds. In fact, when you look at it, it really looks more like the script we would laugh at and say, "Things don't come together that well, right? A full ride to college almost literally handed to you on a silver platter? Come on!"

But that's his story. And the story still ends the same.

## Moving Forward

After finishing the book, I honestly felt a little hopeless and started questioning myself.

Had I done the right things for my students? Did I do enough? What else could I have offered? Did I forget something that could have made the difference? Did I miss the mark because I didn't know them well enough or provide enough feedback or attention in class? Did my attention with some cost me precious time with the others?

For the longest time, I didn't answer the questions. I just left them out there. But I once heard psychologist Adam Sáenz (@AdamLouSaenz) say something along these lines: Educators should feel okay to be worn out by their job. They should be okay with recognizing that at times, we have to pull back to recharge. And they should know that their work is tough and they don't have to be Superman and act like it's not weighing on them. (*If any of that sounds off, I'm sure the mistakes are mine.*) What he said brought me back to my questions, but with different eyes.

As an educator, our work is absolutely going to push us to our limits. Sometimes we discover those limits by giving every last bit of ourselves to the students we serve. We're left with nothing and desperately need to recharge. It's a hard but vital lesson to learn. As teachers, we have to admit exhaustion and take the time and space to rest before we can resume helping our students.

Here's what we can do differently:

1. *Set a goal of relentlessly pursuing and pushing students toward success.* That's what I can control—my end. When I focused on a specific student reaction, not on my role, I equated measurable, meaningful change with a particular response from students. Results aren't something we can control, and our success can't hinge upon something we can't even control.

2. *Believe that all you have to offer is enough.* As it turns out, I just beat myself up about not being enough. I reflected on where I could have done better, but I had no process for helping students work through the same conversation. It wasn't especially helpful for me, and it certainly didn't do anything to help encourage students. They didn't even know. I wish I had helped facilitate a conversation about getting better together.

I'd love it if I were the only person to go through this, but I suspect I'm not alone in wishing I could make more change happen than I was able to see through. I hope your work with students is fruitful, and I hope that in more cases than not, you get to see the fruits of your labor. Remember, it is nearly impossible to THRIVE without opening yourself up to some potential failure. That's okay. Should we approach that flippantly? No. But the work you do as you THRIVE will take you into unmapped territory at times. Doing all you can to reach every student is like that. It's not always a sure bet. But work done to serve every kid in the room is well worth your while. It's what we do when we THRIVE. Every kid deserves to be known and served well at school.

Work done to serve every kid in the room is
well worth your while.
It's what we do when we THRIVE.

That's sometimes easy and sometimes a little riskier. When the risk comes we can get hesitant and start to ask ourselves, "What if I fail?" The failure we sometimes fail to see is the failure that comes by default when we fail to take a risk at all.

## Front Running

Exhaustion is something that I think all educators experience. We express it differently (and often poorly), but it's a nearly inevitable part of our work of service to others. But it's not something we can afford to ignore. Exhaustion is natural, but ultimately it is detrimental to our mission as educators. Still, exhaustion is a part of life with which we are all too familiar.

Growing up, I was a runner. My mom would let me run around and around and around our house until I would just fall down and take a nap just about anywhere (good parenting win there, Mom). But I loved it. I would run a lap around our place and come back and ask if I could run again until my little kid body just couldn't go any more. By the end, I was exhausted, but I didn't start out looking to get exhausted.

I was doing something I enjoyed, which ended up developing a talent in me that would provide the foundation I needed to have fun and build meaningful relationships in cross country and track throughout junior high and high school.

As a young runner, I didn't know much about pacing myself. I would run and run and run and have a blast doing it until I just lost all my energy. As you can imagine, that works for a little while, but as you mature, you learn to manage your energy and conserve it so that you have some left when you need it.

There's a scene I love in the movie *Without Limits*. Bill Bowerman, the Oregon track and Team USA track coach, is sitting down for a coaching session with Steve Prefontaine. Pre, as many knew him, had that front-runner mentality. Always in the front. Always in the lead. Always pushing the pace. Always giving everything he had. For Pre, victory came in outrunning and outlasting your competition.

And it's no exaggeration to say that he was wildly successful doing this. Pre was an Olympian, and he held every record from the 2,000 meters to the 10,000 meters (a *huge* range for those unfamiliar with distance running). A phenomenal talent, his drive, and his plan took him quite far.

But there's a problem with front running: It takes considerably more effort to lead than it does to follow. Drafting behind a runner makes the leader work harder to cut through the wind. But that's a huge mindset shift for someone like Pre, who has always operated out of a different posture with great success.

In the scene I mentioned, Bowerman is trying to convince Pre that there is a better way. Pre states, "I don't want to win unless I've done my best. The only way I know to do that is to run out front and flat out until I have nothing left."

Watching the movie, it's easy to see that a mix of pride and incredible faith in his own talents are holding Pre back. You see, Pre wants to believe there is nothing he can't do. That he lives and runs without limits. Bowerman confronts Pre in a moment of disillusionment and reminds him that, yes, he does have limits, but that he should be thankful for them. They've let him fly pretty high so far.

As an educator, I find myself trying to be that front runner. I want to give it all, to lead with the same mentality Pre had, forgetting that in the end, it wasn't successful for him. It's like I'm wired to push myself toward exhaustion, not in running, but in my work. I know it's not likely to bring the success I want, but it's my natural bent.

And the idea Pre mentioned haunts me a bit: "I don't want to win unless I've done my best. The only way I know to do that is to run out front and flat out until I have nothing left."

When I read it again and think about the amount of energy given to work (even when it's valuable work), I can't help but think about the ways I can see myself trying to adopt the same mindset.

Psychologist Brené Brown wrote that, "When we make the transition from crazy-busy to rest, we have to find out what comforts us, what really refuels us, and do that." And that's what I think we have to do.

Our reality is that we are not enough on our own to be everything that every student needs. We have to be okay with that. With time and reflection on our strengths and lessons learned from our failures, we can get better at this. We can absolutely get better. But this idea that we follow the formula and automatically things work out is a myth. It's out there. I've believed it, and you might have, too. And I don't know that we're going to change that. There's too much outside of our control.

What we can do is think through how we can change ourselves and begin conversations with those around us who are struggling with that feeling of exhaustion and the "I'm not enough" sympathies associated with it.

I wonder how many times I have worn the "exhaustion as a status symbol" as Brown says, and erroneously connecting that with doing my best work. Running flat out in the front until I have nothing left.

I pretend that there is no collateral damage to hitting "empty"— that it's all for the best. But giving everything I have at work leaves me without enough left in the tank to invest at home. I'm not trying to be overly dramatic here. The reality is that if I come home with nothing left, my wife and kids are the ones who lose out.

I'm not at all saying that our work as leaders and change agents isn't worthwhile. The problem is that we have so many worthwhile things pulling on us: school, family, friends, and faith. We owe it to

# We cannot give our all to everything. There's just not enough of us to go around.

---

ourselves and to those we love to make sure the tide isn't pulling us too far in one direction or another.

We cannot give our all to everything. There's just not enough of us to go around. I don't want to end up with nothing left to give in one area of my life. So, here's a start for what we can do to combat that:

- *Identify your pitfalls.*

- *Define your priorities.*

- *Gut check regularly* (preferably with someone else you trust to be honest with you).

Life is too nuanced and unique for me to make hasty generalizations here about how everyone should answer these questions, but I will say this, everyone needs to be asking them, and we all need to be processing these things in the company of those we trust.

Our reality as leaders and change agents is not one that is without limits.

Try as we may to avoid it, you and I will both fail if we do not recognize this reality. Not might. Will.

I can promise it won't be easy, but I can't see energy invested here being anything other than time well spent. The work you are doing and your relationships with others are too important to pretend that you can simply press on without limits.

So before you move on, stop for a minute. Think about the pace you're running at. Is it sustainable? How can it be changed? What would that look like? Is it worth it to you to get it right before you hit your limits?

# My Priorities

My hope for you is that we might be able to identify what really got us into education, and to find ways to do that valuable work we know to be so important for students and teachers. What happened one day that made you know that you wanted to teach? What circumstances presented themselves and affirmed that, yes, you are living out the calling of your life?

As a teacher, I was driven by the belief that students needed a place to belong and that they had an incredible amount to contribute to the world, not only later when they grew up but also right then and there as they sat in my English class as a sophomore or junior in high school.

I sure missed the mark often, but I wish I had gone through this during those years. It would have focused my (rather distracted and sometimes all over the place) work.

In my current role as an assistant principal, I write out some version of this statement as a guide for myself before I start each day: *Make sure everyone on campus feels valued, and equip teachers with what they need to innovate in the classroom.*

Those often fall as those "other duties as assigned" in the job description for an assistant principal, but it's what I value, and I hope it's what helps me do a good job in my work. I'll be the first to say that it seems hokey to say there's so much power in writing it out, but there is. It draws me back to my motivation for pursuing administration, and it forces me to start each day oriented the right way.

Take some time to think back on those first thoughts you had when you felt the call to head down the path toward education. If you've changed roles, what made you pursue this opportunity?

So, really, take some time. Start a watch. Give yourself 10 or 15 minutes to write down what about this work is worth giving your life to. Do it on the next two pages. Writing down your origin story isn't something that can be reined in.

# THRIVE
## SUMMARY QUESTIONS

What do you think about the pace you are moving at right now?

What is good about it?

What might happen if you slowed down or sped up?

What refuels you? Time with others? Time alone? An afternoon with your family? Going somewhere? Staying put?

What do you need to give yourself permission to include in your schedule—not as something separate from your work—but as an essential foundation to your work?

Who or what takes the hit when you hit your exhaustion point?

What steps can you take to make sure you are not overextending yourself?

What are your professional priorities? (If they won't fit in this little space, you need to refine them.)

How can you refocus your energy on your professional priorities?

What are the pitfalls that often pull you in and distract you from the work that really matters most to you?

Put a few "Gut Check" days on your calendar. Try once a week for the next month.

Each day, reflect on how things are going and what you have the power to control in the situation.

# My Hope for You

Teach. And teach well.

On the first day of school, try something you've never tried before. Take a risk. Take a chance. Do something that will stretch you.

Do something crazy. Grade differently. Don't grade at all. Ask the students what they want to learn. Try out that idea you've always wanted to explore—yes, I mean the one you're not sure will work.

Share those ideas you think are ordinary. They'll inspire others more than you know.

Give kids a second chance—not just on the first day, but over and over. They're going to fail (and so will you, and so will I, and it's okay). And when they fail, let them fail, but teach them that failure is part of their learning and part of your learning. It's part of mine.

If your students have never experienced success, make their first steps easy.

If your students have experienced nothing but success, challenge them until they fall on their faces. Their education is incomplete without a chance to learn they can get back up after pushing past their current limits.

In everything you are doing, make the human choice.

Choose to care for a student who is in a tough situation. Choose to help that student be a reader. Choose to help the student who others think doesn't deserve another chance, another shot, another bit of grace. Choose to ask the tough question, to speak that comment you could pass over, to see the best in others, to extend the benefit of the doubt.

And take care of yourself. You're teaching students about how hard it is to balance meaningful work with meaningful relationships in a world where twenty-four hours just don't seem enough and a time turner is almost a necessity.

Teachers—your job is the hardest job I know of. Your desire to do this the right way and your passion for the young people who walk our halls color our school with contagious optimism.

I'm inspired by your dedication and honored to serve students alongside you.

Thank you for all you do. It is most definitely a gift.

# Notes

## Chapter 2

Burgess, Dave. *Teach Like a Pirate*. San Diego, CA: Dave Burgess Consulting, Inc., 2012.

## Chapter 3

@BurgessDave (Dave Burgess), 8 Oct 2015, Twitter, twitter.com/burgessdave/status/655940618057707520

## Chapter 4

McCarthy, Cormac. *The Sunset Limited*. New York, NY: Vintage. 2006.

## Chapter 5

Brown, Brené. "Vulnerability is the birthplace of innovation, creativity and change: Brené Brown at TED2012, *TED Blog*. March 12, 2012. blog.ted.com/vulnerability-is-the-birthplace-of-innovation-creativity-and-change-brene-brown-at-ted2012.

Brown, Brené. *Daring Greatly: How the Courage to Be Vulnerable, Transforms the Way We Live, Love, Parent, and Lead*. New York, NY: Avery. 2012.

## Chapter 6

Roosevelt, Theodore. "Citizenship in a Republic," (Speech), delivered April 23, 1910. design.caltech.edu/erik/Misc/Citizenship_in_a_Republic.pdf.

CHAPTER 9

Hobbs, Jeff. *The Short and Tragic Life of Robert Peace.* New York, NY: Scribner, 2014.

*Without Limits,* directed by Robert Towne (1998, Glendora CA, Warner Bros.).

Cunningham, Lillian. "Exhaustion is not a status symbol," *The Washington Post.* October 3, 2012. washingtonpost.com/national/exhaustion-is-not-a-status-symbol/2012/10/02/19d27aa8-0cba-11e2-bb5e-492c0d30bff6_story.html.

MY HOPE FOR YOU

Inspired by "Leaving a Legacy: Kyle Lake's Message is Alive," *Relevant,* May 30, 2008. archives.relevantmagazine.com/next/blog/6-main-slideshow/206).

# Acknowledgments

My first serious thoughts of writing a book came about a year ago, but the book you're holding is the result of a lot of investment from others over a much longer time frame. Without each of these influences, there is no way that this book would be here.

First and foremost, to my wife, Emily, thank you for all of your patience and support for the past ten years. Thank you for all you have taken on to help provide space for this book to come together. I love our little family, and I'm so thankful to be walking through each day with you.

To my parents and my sister, thank you for teaching me what ultimately matters in life through your words and actions every day. Your example has shaped me more than you know, and I'm so thankful that Graham, James, and Joy get to spend so much time with each of you learning the same. I hit the family jackpot.

To my church leaders growing up, thank you for investing in that quiet, nerdy kid who kept showing up every time the doors were open. You built a firm foundation of faith in me and were the first to really teach me the value of questioning "the way we've always done it."

To the A&M Consolidated High School English department (and all the other people who end up at Mike's Christmas party each year—you know who you are), I'm beyond thankful to have learned how to be a teacher from all of you. Thank you for welcoming me in and showing me how to handle all the challenges that teaching can throw at you.

To all my colleagues at AMCHS and Cypress Grove, you set the bar so high for what it looks like to love coming to work to serve students well. I couldn't have asked for two better places to serve, and I'm thankful to serve alongside so many amazing educators each day.

To my PLN, thank you for all of the ways you challenge and support me. The past few years have been filled with amazing growth, and that wouldn't have happened without you all. Special thanks go out to the #LeadUpChat and #CSISDchat communities for the way you push me to reflect and grow as a professional. Thank you for giving of yourself in that space. It's made a profound impact on me.

To Jeremy Stewart and Jeff Mann, thank you for all of the conversations about everything over the past couple of years. Your insights make me better every day, and I will always be grateful for you both.

To Dave and Shelley Burgess, thank you for believing in this message and bringing this book from idea into reality.

And to that persistent handful of people who kept on asking, "When are you going to write a book?" despite my dismissive responses, thank you for continuing to ask. It seems to have paid off.

# Bring Aaron Hogan to Your School or Event

Aaron Hogan draws on his experience as both a teacher and an administrator to design keynotes and workshops that actually make a difference for educators. Whether it's on campus or sharing at a conference, professional development with Aaron offers a mix of challenges to push you out of your comfort zone and into the growth that will shatter the perfect teacher myth and help you THRIVE.

## Popular Keynotes and Workshops

THRIVE

Lead So Teachers Will THRIVE

Blogging IS Learning: Making Time to Reflect & Grow

Get Connected: Rejecting Isolation as Educators

Edcamp Your PD: Creating Simple Personalized PD

Create Space to Connect: Launching a District Twitter Chat

Learn more about these keynotes and sessions, see where Aaron will be speaking soon, or book him for your school or event at
***afhogan.com/speaking***

# More From

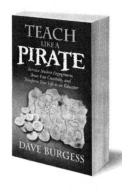

# Dave Burgess
## Consulting, Inc.

### Teach Like a PIRATE
*Increase Student Engagement, Boost Your Creativity, and Transform Your Life as an Educator*
By Dave Burgess (@BurgessDave)

*Teach Like a PIRATE* is the *New York Times'* best-selling book that has sparked a worldwide educational revolution. It is part inspirational manifesto that ignites passion for the profession, and part practical road map filled with dynamic strategies to dramatically increase student engagement. Translated into multiple languages, its message resonates with educators who want to design outrageously creative lessons and transform school into a life-changing experience for students.

### P is for PIRATE
*Inspirational ABC's for Educators*
By Dave and Shelley Burgess (@Burgess_Shelley)

Teaching is an adventure that stretches the imagination and calls for creativity every day! In *P is for PIRATE*, husband and wife team Dave and Shelley Burgess encourage and inspire educators to make their classrooms fun and exciting places to learn. Tapping into years of personal experience and drawing on the insights of more than seventy educators, the authors offer a wealth of ideas for making learning and teaching more fulfilling than ever before.

### Learn Like a PIRATE
*Empower Your Students to Collaborate, Lead, and Succeed*
By Paul Solarz (@PaulSolarz)

Today's job market demands that students be prepared to take responsibility for their lives and careers. We do them a disservice if we teach them how to earn passing grades without equipping them to take charge of their education. In *Learn Like a PIRATE*, Paul Solarz explains how to design classroom experiences that encourage students to take risks and explore their passions in a stimulating, motivating, and supportive environment where improvement, rather than grades, is the focus. Discover how student-led classrooms help students thrive and develop into self-directed, confident citizens who are capable of making smart, responsible decisions, all on their own.

### Play Like a Pirate
*Engage Students with Toys, Games, and Comics*
By Quinn Rollins (@jedikermit)

Yes! Serious learning can be seriously fun. In *Play Like a Pirate*, Quinn Rollins offers practical, engaging strategies and resources that make it easy to integrate fun into your curriculum. Regardless of the grade level you teach, you'll find inspiration and ideas that will help you engage your students in unforgettable ways.

## eXPlore Like a Pirate

*Gamification and Game-Inspired Course Design to Engage, Enrich, and Elevate Your Learners*

By Michael Matera (@MrMatera)

Are you ready to transform your classroom into an experiential world that flourishes on collaboration and creativity? Then set sail with classroom game designer and educator Michael Matera as he reveals the possibilities and power of game-based learning. In *eXPlore Like a Pirate*, Matera serves as your experienced guide to help you apply the most motivational techniques of game play to your classroom. You'll learn gamification strategies that will work with and enhance (rather than replace) your current curriculum and discover how these engaging methods can be applied to any grade level or subject.

## Lead Like a PIRATE

*Make School Amazing for Your Students and Staff*

By Shelley Burgess and Beth Houf (@Burgess_Shelley, @BethHouf)

In *Lead Like a PIRATE*, education leaders Shelley Burgess and Beth Houf map out the character traits necessary to captain a school or district. You'll learn where to find the treasure that's already in your classrooms and schools—and how to bring out the very best in your educators. This book will equip and encourage you to be relentless in your quest to make school amazing for your students, staff, parents, and communities.

## The Innovator's Mindset

*Empower Learning, Unleash Talent, and Lead a Culture of Creativity*
By George Couros (@gcouros)

The traditional system of education requires students to hold their questions and compliantly stick to the scheduled curriculum. But our job as educators is to provide new and better opportunities for our students. It's time to recognize that compliance doesn't foster innovation, encourage critical thinking, or inspire creativity—and those are the skills our students need to succeed. In *The Innovator's Mindset*, George Couros encourages teachers and administrators to empower their learners to wonder, to explore—and to become forward-thinking leaders.

## Shift This!

*How to Implement Gradual Changes for MASSIVE Impact in Your Classroom*
By Joy Kirr

Establishing a student-led culture that isn't focused on grades and homework but on individual responsibility and personalized learning, may seem like a daunting task—especially if you think you have to do it all at once. But significant change is possible, sustainable, and even easy when it happens little by little. In *Shift This!* educator and speaker Joy Kirr explains how to make gradual shifts—in your thinking, teaching, and approach to classroom design—that will have a massive impact in your classroom. Make the first shift today!

## *LAUNCH*

*Using Design Thinking to Boost Creativity and Bring Out the Maker in Every Student*
By John Spencer and A.J. Juliani
(@spencerideas, @ajjuliani)

Something happens in students when they define themselves as makers and inventors and creators. They discover powerful skills—problem solving, critical thinking, and imagination—that will help them shape the world's future ... our future. In *LAUNCH*, John Spencer and A.J. Juliani provide a process that can be incorporated into every class at every grade level ... even if you don't consider yourself a "creative teacher." And if you dare to innovate and view creativity as an essential skill, you will empower your students to change the world—starting right now.

## *Pure Genius*

*Building a Culture of Innovation and Taking 20% Time to the Next Level*
By Don Wettrick (@DonWettrick)

For far too long, schools have been bastions of boredom, killers of creativity, and way too comfortable with compliance and conformity. In *Pure Genius*, Don Wettrick explains how collaboration—with experts, students, and other educators—can help you create interesting, and even life-changing, opportunities for learning. Wettrick's book inspires and equips educators with a systematic blueprint for teaching innovation in any school.

## *Teaching Math with Google Apps*

*50 G Suite Activities*

By Alice Keeler and Diana Herrington
(@AliceKeeler, @mathdiana)

Google Apps give teachers the opportunity to interact with students in a more meaningful way than ever before, while G Suite empowers students to be creative, critical thinkers who collaborate as they explore and learn. In *Teaching Math with Google Apps*, educators Alice Keeler and Diana Herrington demonstrate fifty different ways to bring math classes to the twenty-first century with easy-to-use technology.

## *Table Talk Math*

*A Practical Guide for Bringing Math into Everyday Conversations*

By John Stevens (@Jstevens009)

Making math part of families' everyday conversations is a powerful way to help children and teens learn to love math. In *Table Talk Math*, John Stevens offers parents (and teachers!) ideas for initiating authentic, math-based conversations that will get kids to notice and be curious about all the numbers, patterns, and equations in the world around them.

## The Classroom Chef

*Sharpen your lessons. Season your classes. Make math meaningful.*

By John Stevens and Matt Vaudrey (@Jstevens009, @MrVaudrey)

In *The Classroom Chef*, math teachers and instructional coaches John Stevens and Matt Vaudrey share their secret recipes, ingredients, and tips for serving up lessons that engage students and help them "get" math. You can use these ideas and methods as-is, or better yet, tweak them and create your own enticing educational meals. The message the authors share is that, with imagination and preparation, every teacher can be a Classroom Chef.

## Instant Relevance

*Using Today's Experiences in Tomorrow's Lessons*

By Denis Sheeran (@MathDenisNJ)

Every day, students in schools around the world ask the question, "When am I ever going to use this in real life?" In *Instant Relevance*, author and keynote speaker Denis Sheeran equips you to create engaging lessons from experiences and events that matter to your students. Learn how to help your students see meaningful connections between the real world and what they learn in the classroom—because that's when learning sticks.

## 50 Things You Can Do with Google Classroom

By Alice Keeler and Libbi Miller
(@alicekeeler, @MillerLibbi)

It can be challenging to add new technology to the classroom, but it's a must if students are going to be well-equipped for the future. Alice Keeler and Libbi Miller shorten the learning curve by providing a thorough overview of the Google Classroom App. Part of Google Apps for Education (GAfE), Google Classroom was specifically designed to help teachers save time by streamlining the process of going digital. Complete with screenshots, *50 Things You Can Do with Google Classroom* provides ideas and step-by-step instructions to help teachers implement this powerful tool.

## 50 Things to Go Further with Google Classroom

*A Student-Centered Approach*
By Alice Keeler and Libbi Miller
(@alicekeeler, @MillerLibbi)

Today's technology empowers educators to move away from the traditional classroom where teachers lead and students work independently—each doing the same thing. In *50 Things to Go Further with Google Classroom: A Student-Centered Approach*, authors and educators Alice Keeler and Libbi Miller offer inspiration and resources to help you create a digitally rich, engaging, student-centered environment. They show you how to tap into the power of individualized learning that is possible with Google Classroom.

## *140 Twitter Tips for Educators*

*Get Connected, Grow Your Professional Learning Network, and Reinvigorate Your Career*

By Brad Currie, Billy Krakower, and Scott Rocco (@bradmcurrie, @wkrakower, @ScottRRocco)

Whatever questions you have about education or about how you can be even better at your job, you'll find ideas, resources, and a vibrant network of professionals ready to help you on Twitter. In *140 Twitter Tips for Educators*, #Satchat hosts and founders of Evolving Educators, Brad Currie, Billy Krakower, and Scott Rocco offer step-by-step instructions to help you master the basics of Twitter, build an online following, and become a Twitter rock star.

## *Ditch That Textbook*

*Free Your Teaching and Revolutionize Your Classroom*
By Matt Miller (@jmattmiller)

Textbooks are symbols of centuries of old education. They're often outdated as soon as they hit students' desks. Acting "by the textbook" implies compliance and a lack of creativity. It's time to ditch those textbooks—and those textbook assumptions about learning! In *Ditch That Textbook*, teacher and blogger Matt Miller encourages educators to throw out meaningless, pedestrian teaching and learning practices. He empowers them to evolve and improve on old, standard teaching methods. *Ditch That Textbook* is a support system, toolbox, and manifesto to help educators free their teaching and revolutionize their classrooms.

## *Your School Rocks ... So Tell People!*

*Passionately Pitch and Promote the Positives Happening on Your Campus*

By Ryan McLane and Eric Lowe
(@McLane_Ryan, @EricLowe21)

Great things are happening in your school every day. The problem is, no one beyond your school walls knows about them. School principals Ryan McLane and Eric Lowe want to help you get the word out! In *Your School Rocks ... So Tell People!* McLane and Lowe offer more than seventy immediately actionable tips along with easy-to-follow instructions and links to video tutorials. This practical guide will equip you to create an effective and manageable communication strategy using social-media tools. Learn how to keep your students' families and community connected, informed, and excited about what's going on in your school.

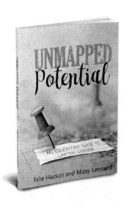

## *Unmapped Potential*

*An Educator's Guide to Lasting Change*

By Julie Hasson and Missy Lennard
(@PPrincipals)

No matter where you are in your educational career, chances are you have, at times, felt overwhelmed and overworked. Maybe you feel that way right now. If so, you aren't alone. But the more important news is that things can get better! You simply need the right map to guide you from frustrated to fulfilled. *Unmapped Potential* offers advice and practical strategies to help you find your unique path to becoming the kind of educator—the kind of person—you want to be.

## The Zen Teacher
*Creating FOCUS, SIMPLICITY, and TRANQUILITY in the Classroom*
By Dan Tricarico (@thezenteacher)

Teachers have incredible power to influence, even improve, the future. In *The Zen Teacher*, educator, blogger, and speaker Dan Tricarico provides practical, easy-to-use techniques to help teachers be their best—unrushed and fully focused—so they can maximize their performance and improve their quality of life. In this introductory guide, Dan Tricarico explains what it means to develop a Zen practice—something that has nothing to do with religion and everything to do with your ability to thrive in the classroom.

## How Much Water Do We Have?
*5 Success Principles for Conquering Any Change and Thriving in Times of Change*
By Pete Nunweiler with Kris Nunweiler

In *How Much Water Do We Have?* Pete Nunweiler identifies five key elements that are necessary for the success of any goal, life transition, or challenge: information, planning, motivation, support, and leadership. Referring to these elements as the 5 Waters of Success, Pete explains that, like the water we drink, you need them to thrive in today's rapidly paced world. If you're feeling stressed out, overwhelmed, or uncertain at work or at home, pause and look for the signs of dehydration. Learn how to find, acquire, and use the 5 Waters of Success—so you can share them with your team and family members.

## The Writing on the Classroom Wall

*How Posting Your Most Passionate Beliefs about Education Can Empower Your Students, Propel Your Growth, and Lead to a Lifetime of Learning*

By Steve Wyborney (@SteveWyborney)

In *The Writing on the Classroom Wall*, Steve Wyborney explains how posting and discussing Big Ideas can lead to deeper learning. You'll learn why sharing your ideas will sharpen and refine them. You'll also be encouraged to know that the Big Ideas you share don't have to be profound to make a profound impact on learning. In fact, Steve explains, it's okay if some of your ideas fall off the wall. What matters most is sharing them.

## Kids Deserve It!

*Pushing Boundaries and Challenging Conventional Thinking*

By Todd Nesloney and Adam Welcome (@TechNinjaTodd, @awelcome)

In *Kids Deserve It!*, Todd and Adam encourage you to think big and make learning fun and meaningful for students. Their high-tech, high-touch, and highly engaging practices will inspire you to take risks, shake up the status quo, and be a champion for your students. While you're at it, you just might rediscover why you became an educator in the first place.

## Escaping the School Leader's Dunk Tank

*How to Prevail When Others Want to See You Drown*

By Rebecca Coda and Rick Jetter

(@RebeccaCoda, @RickJetter)

No school leader is immune to the effects of discrimination, bad politics, revenge, or ego-driven coworkers. These kinds of dunk-tank situations can make an educator's life miserable. By sharing real-life stories and insightful research, the authors (who are dunk-tank survivors themselves) equip school leaders with the practical knowledge and emotional tools necessary to survive and, better yet, avoid getting "dunked."

## Start. Right. Now.

*Teach and Lead for Excellence*

By Todd Whitaker, Jeff Zoul, and Jimmy Casas

(@ToddWhitaker, @Jeff_Zoul, @casas_jimmy)

In their work leading up to *Start. Right. Now.* Todd Whitaker, Jeff Zoul, and Jimmy Casas studied educators from across the nation and discovered four key behaviors of excellence: Excellent leaders and teachers Know the Way, Show the Way, Go the Way, and Grow Each Day. If you are ready to take the first step toward excellence, this motivating book will put you on the right path.

## Master the Media

*How Teaching Media Literacy Can Save Our Plugged-in World*

By Julie Smith

Written to help teachers and parents educate the next generation, *Master the Media* explains the history, purpose, and messages behind the media. The point isn't to get kids to unplug; it's to help them make informed choices, understand the difference between truth and lies, and discern perception from reality. Critical thinking leads to smarter decisions—and it's why media literacy can save the world.

## Social LEADia

*How Teaching Media Literacy Can Save Our Plugged-in World*

By Jennifer Casa-Todd

Equipping students for their future begins by helping them become digital leaders *now*. In our networked society, students need to learn how to leverage social media to connect to people, passions, and opportunities to grow and make a difference. *Social LEADia* addresses the need to shift the conversations at school and at home from digital citizenship to *digital leadership*.

# About the Author

Aaron Hogan is a husband, a dad of three, and an educator who is committed to helping those around him be their best. Since he entered the classroom nine years ago as a high school English teacher, he has been trying to reimagine education within his sphere of influence to make school great for students. He currently serves as an assistant principal at Cypress Grove Intermediate School in College Station, Texas. He previously served in the same district as an assistant principal and classroom teacher at his alma mater, A&M Consolidated High School.

In addition, Aaron is a blogger, author, and speaker. He is passionate about social emotional learning, innovation in education, and connecting educators for professional growth. Aaron is the co-creator of #CSISDchat, a weekly Twitter chat that seeks to provide space for educators to connect with, challenge, and support one another (join the conversation Tuesdays at 8 p.m. CST).

 @aaron_hogan

 @aaronfhogan

 afhogan.com

CPSIA information can be obtained
at www.ICGtesting.com
Printed in the USA
FFOW02n1519110617
36572FF